My Life Story

Led by the Fathers Hand...

Soli Deo Gloria
to God be the Glory
Elisabeth Star Lehotsky

By Elisabeth Star Lehotsky

Preface

From Yugoslavia as a Refugee to the Promised Land – USA

It was a Sunday just before midnight when I was born on September 29, 1940. Now that I am 79 I will try to record my life story at the urging of my children before senior moments take away the most precious memories. By no means do I consider myself a "writer", but by the Grace of God I will recall my life journey. It is my prayer that the reader can see my heavenly Fathers hand leading me throughout my life. To Him be all the Honor and Glory.

Chapter One
Early History

I have to go back to start with my family's history on my mother's side. Back in the eighteen-hundreds the Pfann Family migrated from Alsace-Lorraine, an Imperial German Territory, down into Croatia/Slavonia and Serbia along the Danube River, Batschka and Banat. They were called "Donau Schwaben" – Danube Swabians. The land was very fertile, and the German immigrants were very industrious. They became rich land owners.

The Gasteiger family, my grandfather's side, came from the Salzburg a province in Austria. Josef Gasteiger married Christine Pfann and they had a daughter Maria, born January 10, 1919, and a son Viktor, born September 24, 1926. Maria was my mother, and she married my father Johann Star, who was the son of Johann and Theresie Sic Star.

Born into a Christian family was not a "given" but a blessing, that started when a group of Christians from Ridgewood/Brooklyn, New York began a mission trip to Croatia. They were immigrants to the USA from Croatia, and had joined an established German speaking Pentecostal church in New York.

The spreading of the gospel resulted in a revival when most of my mother's extended family were saved. She was only twelve years old when she realized her need to have her sins forgiven and accept Jesus as her Savior. The new Christians were baptized by immersion and became members of the Pentecostal church. However, they did not baptize children, and Mom had to wait to prove that her conversion was real. She was then baptized by immersion.

When her Family moved to the capital city of Croatia called Agram in German, Zagreb in Croatian, my mom became an apprentice seamstress. Her desire to study music was denied, because in those days a girl had to learn to sew, cook, keep a neat house, and become a wife and mother. The family attended an already established Baptist church where she met Johann Star, my father, a devout Christian. Coming from a strong Catholic background, he was led to the Lord by his boss when he was an apprentice carpenter making fine furniture. He was baptized by immersion and joined the Baptist church.

That church is still there, alive and well today. I will tell about it later on. They were married on April 3, 1937, and served the Lord together with their talents. My father played the violin and Mom the organ. My mother had a beautiful soprano voice and my dad a bass/baritone. They sang together, and at times my dad would also preach. Music played a large part in our family life. My sister Lydia was born on March 18, 1938, in Zagreb/Agram. The family moved back to Vinkovci when I came along on Sunday just before midnight on September 29, 1940, Erika in April 24, 1942, and the youngest, Frieda in February 9, 1944.

My mother had her hands full, especially with me. I once was caught with scissors trying to cut my hair before I was three years old. When visitors came, they would tease me that I forgot to wash my eyes. You see I had very blond curly hair, and my dark brown eyes stood out. One day when a visitor teased me again, I stumped to the wash basin, grabbed the scrub brush, and started toward my eyes, when my mom grabbed me to prevent injury to my eyes. From then on, no one teased me again.

I remember when my dad came home. I was allowed to sit on his lap, with Lydia on the other side. Dad had made a table just for us children to eat on, and a very sturdy kitchen table for the grownups. He was very loving but strict, insisting that we speak German, which I resisted because I wanted to speak Croatian, like all the other kids in our neighborhood, so I got many spankings before learning to obey.

World War II was raging. When Hitler marched into Yugoslavia, all men of German descent were drafted into the German Army. Being that my Dad was a strong Christian and did not want to kill anyone, he was allowed to serve at the hospital and frequently came home to Vinkovci.

One day a German officer came to the house and wanted to take up residence. When my Mom resisted, being a young woman with four little girls, he pulled his gun out and aimed it at her while we little ones screamed. Just before pulling the trigger he asked where my father was. When she told him where he was stationed, he said, "That saved your life," for he would have shot her down as an enemy of the German Reich. Then he left. I know it was the Lord that made that officer stop and ask that question.

Other traumatic memories were of the air raid sirens and the whistling sounds of the falling bombs. We did not have an air raid shelter, so mom grabbed us girls huddling under the kitchen table, and then she raced to open all windows to keep the glass from shattering from the fallout.

Hunger was also an issue. Mom did not have enough milk to nurse the baby, so she just browned some flour in a little oil and poured water over it to keep her baby alive. My grandfather gave me a black angora hare (domesticated rabbit) for my fourth birthday. I kept him on a string tied down in the back yard. Hunger was such a problem, Mom put him on a wood chopping log, and with the axe chopped his head off to make rabbit stew for us to eat.

Chapter Two
Evacuation

All Germans were evacuated from Croatia when the Red Army, the Russians, advanced and it became evident that the Germans were on the losing side. My mom did not want to leave. Where was she to go? A young woman of 25 with four little girls ages six, four, two, and an eight-month-old baby. How was she able to keep us all together?

My dad came home one day, packed us up, and forcefully took us to the last train that pulled out of Croatia in October 1944. He knew that we were in danger and had to leave, for the partisans were killing any Germans, even civilians. My maternal grandmother came with us, so there were at least two women to hold us together on the overcrowded train. I still remember the tearful goodbyes, clinging to my dad. I did not know that that would be the last time we would see my dad alive.

We were taken northeast across Hungary and Czechoslovakia into East Germany. Periodically the train was stopped by the enemy soldiers, who took women off the train to rape them. But the Lord's hand was on my mom, who was hiding under my grandmother's long dress. We reached East Germany at Falkenstein near Plauen, and were put up in a university building. We had to sleep on lice infested straw on the floor of the class rooms, where wave after wave of refugees had slept. My mother had her hands full trying to free us girls from the lice in our hair.

My grandfather who had worked for the railroad, writing timetables by hand, was able to secure a railroad car to bring some of our belongings out of Croatia. My dad had packed up some of our belongings, mom's treadle sewing machine, and our featherbeds as well as some warm clothing. He also packed family pictures and even some German hymn books that had been donated by a German speaking Baptist church in America. How my grandfather found us there in East Germany I do not know, but I'm sure the Lord had his hand in it. Those hymnals made it full circle back to America with us. I still have those hymn books.

Night after night the air raid sirens went off and we scrambled to get to the shelters. One time we did not make it fast enough to the shelter when the planes started to drop the bombs. Mom tried to take shelter at the door of a house and was chased away by the owners. They hurled insults at us, "You dirty refugees, go home, you came to eat our bread away!" Decent people became vicious because of the war.

One night when the sirens were blaring, we were running to the air raid shelter again, my great grandfather could no longer run because of his heart condition, so he stayed behind with his wife. The building took a hit. Both of his legs were cut off in two places and he died on the spot. His wife got shrapnel in her knee. She survived, but with a stiff leg for the rest of her life. When we returned, we saw the building cut in half, and you could look into the class rooms where my great grandfather was killed.

There was a crater from the bomb in the yard with debris and lots of broken glass. My two-year-old sister Erika fell into it, and she still has a scar on the back of her leg that looks like a run in the stocking. The continuous trauma was just too much for her, and she started screaming. She could not stop for hours and days. She was taken to a hospital and diagnosed with a nerve fever. We contracted all kinds of childhood diseases, and my sister Lydia even had scarlet fever.

In 1945 the Russians were advancing, and we were in danger again. After nine months in East Germany, we were packed into open cattle trains and shipped out. Then the war was over, we tried to return back home to Croatia. Our route took us through Czechoslovakia, into Austria. Outside Vienna we encountered another problem. The railroad bridge over the Danube River was bombed out.

Romans 8:28 *"For we know that all things work together for good to those who love God and are called according to His purpose."*

The Lord used this incident to keep us in Austria, for we later heard that the refugees on trains that made it to the border of Yugoslavia, were captured and taken into Russian concentration camps. Only a few survived to tell the story. Now we were stranded on the open road for three weeks. There was no food, and we were starving. People scoured the surrounding fields that had been harvested, to find something to eat. Someone found a pile of potatoes, and everyone was rushing to get some. However, they were found to be rotten. You can imagine the smell of a pile of rotten potatoes. That did not stop my mom and others to try to find any solid pieces. With maggots crawling up mom's legs and arms, she desperately tried to find some solid pieces to feed her starving children.

After three weeks the leader of our transport found a way to get into the city of Vienna on foot. We were taken into a detention camp, but it was in the Russian zone. Austria, including the capital city, was occupied and divided by the allies into four zones.

At the camp was a Russian guard who knew that my mom had four little girls. Mom spoke fluent Russian, and he told my mom that he would help us get out of that camp, because the Russians planned to ship all able-bodied persons to Siberia to hard labor camps, and she would be one of them. He told Mom not to say anything to anyone, for he would be killed if the word got out. Mom asked him why he was taking that chance to help us, he replied that he had a wife and four little girls back in Russia. He was praying that God would protect them and bring him back to them as a reward for this good deed. The night that he was on guard duty he would turn his back to us, so we could escape.

With the help of a Baptist church, we were able to find lodging in the basement of a private house. The refugees had to either work by removing the rubble of the badly bombed city, or go into the Vienna woods to cut down huge trees by hand for lumber. Mom chose to work in the woods, and the Lord was gracious to get her to work for a boss that treated her kindly. My grandmother had to take care of us four little girls.

I remember how glad she was to get some food for us to cook, even though it was only dried peas, however they were old and had bugs in them. She soaked them over night and we had to pick the bugs out the next day, then she cooked them. When she was able to get some onions, she taught us how to peel only the outer skin, as not to lose any of the precious onion.

Chapter Three
Keeping Family Together

The winter of 1945/46 was one of the worst in recorded history. Mom did not have any warm clothing. She wore my father's pants, but that did not protect her enough from the waist high snow. She got a kidney infection, and there was no way to get proper medical treatment. She later died of kidney failure, on the day before her 42nd birthday in 1961, here in America.

Her boss had an elderly father who needed someone to cut firewood for him. So, on her day off, Mom went to work for the old man. In return her boss gave her a pair of shoes that his son had outgrown. Lydia needed the shoes to start school. When the Russians ordered that all refugees had to register, the Lord used Mom's boss who told her not to go and register, but to get out of the Russian zone. The Russians were taking all able-bodied people and shipping them to Siberia to hard labor camps. They just tore families apart. There were thousands of children without any parents, and we would have been among them.

The Lord spared us the horror of being separated as a family. Everyone wanted to get out of the Russian zone. Mom took us girls and reached the neighboring British zone. She went to the see the officer in charge, begging to take us in. He sadly told her there was no room, for everyone wanted to get out of the Russian zone. In desperation she grabbed the gun on his desk, and said she would shoot her girls in front of him and also herself, for she would not, could not go back into the Russian zone. The officer relented and sent us to a refugee camp in the southern part of Austria. It was the province of Kärnten/Carinthia that was under the British occupation.

The former prisoner of war camp in Kärnten was turned into a refugee camp. The barracks had no partitions, chalk lines were drawn on the floor for the allotted space, and blankets were used for privacy. There was no insulation, and the Austrian winters were severe. With no warm clothing, we had to stay indoors. I contracted pneumonia that left a shadow on my lungs. That condition later caused us to delay our immigration to the America. We received 25 grams of hard bread, a little less than one ounce, and some thin soup for our daily ration. We were starving! Our women went to the surrounding farms, trading anything of value like wedding bands or jewelry just for a few potatoes.

Mom's ill-fitting shoes caused a blister on her heal and she got blood poisoning. The red stripe was already up her leg when she was taken to the camp infirmary. She overheard two doctors arguing over the last penicillin shot. One wanted to save it for "their" people (there were refugees of all different nationalities in that camp) the other one wanted to save my mother's life. The Lord intervened and Mom was spared for her children.

The administration barracks had pictures posted of hundreds of children who were left without parents. Some of them did not even know their names. The Red Cross was desperately trying to reunite families. My grandfather had a radio, and when the Red Cross announced the names of people who searched for their family members, every one gathered around to listen for the name of their loved ones. I remember listening to the announcer call out names, he started to say: Johann St... and stopped. I was so excited that my dad was looking for us, but the man just continued on without calling my father's last name, Johann Star.

Even though the war had ended, the suffering continued on. Soldiers returning from the war were coming through the camp looking for their families. One day a soldier came by our barracks looking for his family. When the elderly couple across our chalk line saw that he had only thin torn pants on, they called him in to give him some clothes from their son who had previously immigrated to Canada. Everyone wanted to know where he came from and where he was stationed. It turned out that he was in the same battalion with my dad. They asked if he knew where my dad was. He said, "Yes."

My dad was with a group of ten other soldiers searching the railroad tracks for booby traps. They were captured by partisans, lined up and mowed down by bullets. My mom screamed, and we children started to cry. The poor man was so shocked when he heard that we were the family of Johann Star, that he just grabbed the clothes and left in a hurry. We never even got his name, and my mom had to wait five years to get the death certificate.

The conditions in the camp were not getting any better. Tuberculosis spread through the camp like wildfire and our malnourished bodies were in danger of contracting it. Mom was afraid for us but she relied on God's promises.

Jeremiah 29: 11 *"For I know the plan I have for you declares the Lord, plans not for evil but to give you a future and a hope."*

Some refugees who had relatives in the USA and Canada were able to immigrate to those countries. Others found work on farms, and Mom tried that too, but with four little children and only one worker, no farmer would take us. When word got out that my mom had a sewing machine, Paul Folschan, a tailor, asked to use it. He too was a former prisoner of war. When he saw that we children did not have any warm clothing, he made us coats, and pants from old horse blankets. He even made us shoes, using the rubber from old truck tires for the soles. He fell in love with Mom, and they eventually got married. They had two girls, Christine and Maria. So now I had a stepfather and two more sisters. Mom's parents also came along to care for us children. Because of my grandfather's poor health, he could not work, so he was not drafted into the German military.

Chapter Four
Life on the Farm

Now that we had two workers, a farmer was found who was willing to take us in. I'll never forget when we arrived, the farmer's wife brought us a BIG bowl of cream of wheat cooked in milk. We devoured that special treat, and it brought tears to the farmer's wife, watching us lick the bowl dry.

I do not remember why we went to another farm later on, but that farmer was cruel. Our sleeping quarters were above the pig sty. Mom had to get up at 3am to slop the pigs, milk seven cows by hand, and be on the field at 7am. They worked in the fields all day, only to return back to the barn to slop the pigs, and milk the cows again. Mom, having been raised in the capital city, quickly had to learn how to milk cows by hand. When the time came to get her wages, the farmer told her that we ate more than she had earned. We then moved to another farm. There were nine of us now, four adults and five children. This time we got a big room above the horse stable, and the food was better.

We went to school in the nearby town. It was difficult for we only spoke our German dialect. Having missed so much schooling, we had a lot of catching up to do in our respective grades. Our German was spoken in a dialect, and we had to learn the proper German as well. I was impressed by the cross in front of the class room, and the teacher leading us in the Lord's Prayer before class started. Religious instruction was also part of the curriculum.

I remember when the Catholic priest came to class and showed a picture of the Lord's last supper, and said that the children who went through the first communion will each receive a picture like that. I was not Catholic, but I wanted a picture so bad, that I went to confession, a requirement. I searched my brain to find something that I could confess to the priest, as a seven-year-old child I did not understand sin. All I could think of that one day I stole a sugar cube from my grandmother's sugar bowl. For that sin I had to recite ten Lord's Prayers and ten Ave Marias. I knelt on the cold steps near the altar and faithfully recited them. But then, when it came time for the first communion I could not participate because I was not Catholic. Needless to say, I did not receive that picture.

In school the girls had to learn to knit and crochet as part of the curriculum, but we did not have any wool. Old sweaters were used and unraveled so we could have wool to learn with.

Chapter Five
Switzerland

When I was in third grade the Red Cross sent someone to choose two refugee children from the school, to go to Switzerland where families opened their homes for three months to the starved refugee children. Here again the Lord had his hands on me, for I was one of the two chosen.

I was placed into a loving family in the German speaking part of Switzerland. The daughter of that family came to Zurich where the distribution place was. She was expecting to pick up a boy, but instead got me. I was to go to a family in the French speaking part of Switzerland, but the Lord had other plans for me. While waiting at the train station I started to cry for my mother. The daughter of my Swiss family tried to console me, bought me a big bar of Swiss chocolates. I had never seen chocolate before. I just kept on crying. She told me that she would call my mom. I was so naïve, that I believed her. She did get on the phone, but it was to call her parents to tell them that she would bring a girl.

The train ride was exciting to me, for it was nothing like the trains we were put on as evacuees. The countryside was beautiful like in Austria. The whole town of Kuettigen accepted me as "their child". The family was very good to me. When I told them that I had four more sisters at home, and that we slept two and two in twin beds on straw mattresses, they collected clothing, beddings, and toys in a 50-lb box and sent it to our home in Austria.

At their house I had a featherbed to sleep on and a feather covering on top to snuggle under. When it was time to eat, I was fed two breakfasts, two lunches and two suppers, for the neighbors that provided the food, ate at different times, and I drank goats milk. They wanted to fatten me up before I had to return back to Austria.

I quickly learned the Swiss dialect which was very different from ours. But in school everyone had to speak proper German. A neighbor's girl and I competed with knitting. It was wonderful to have new wool to work with. I have pictures of the two of us. She was almost twice the size of me.

I loved that family. We played games, did knitting, and we sang together. I remember the deep bass voice the father had. When there was a wedding, we lined the streets, as the bus with the wedding party came through. Everyone on the bus was throwing individual wrapped candy out the windows for us to pick up.

Another thing that impressed me was the tiled stove that reached from the floor to the ceiling with a bench to sit on in the living room. It was heated by the kitchen wood stove on the other side of the wall.

In Switzerland all young and older men had to serve in the army and be on reserve duty all their lives. One day they came to our town on maneuvers. I went ballistic! I thought that the war was on again, and I was not with my mom and sisters. The family could barely hold me down I was so hysterical. When the planes flew overhead I associated it with the war planes, and waited to hear the whistling sound of the bombs falling. That too passed, and it gave my Swiss family an insight of the trauma I had gone through.

Then it was time to return to the refugee camp in Austria.

For over 60 years I have stayed in contact by mail with those loving people in Switzerland.

Chapter Six
Back to the Refugee Camp

Not long after I returned from Switzerland, my grandmother died from complications of gallbladder surgery. Her heart just could not take it. She was only 49 years old. So now there was no one to take care of us children while Mom worked, and the farmer kicked us out. We needed to go back to the refugee camp. Because of the overcrowded conditions, we were denied entrance. The Lord's intervention was evident, for my mother's brother was taken by the British to work for them as a driver to the commanding officer. That good man used his influence to get us a place in the camp.

By now the barracks had partitions. Rooms were assigned according to the size of the family. We still had to stand in line at the soup kitchen and take our daily dose of cod liver oil. To this day I can't stand the smell of fish without remembering that oily fishy stuff.

The health department used a beautiful castle above the Millstaetter See to house refugee children for one week at a time. My sister Erika and I were among them and had the most wonderful time. There was lots of good food and many children to play with. One day the president of Austria Dr. Karl Renner came for a visit, and we had to stand at attention. We were in awe of him. We sang for him and his entourage.

The following year two neighboring Swiss families got together to privately bring me back to Switzerland for another three months. The towns people still considered me as "their" child. They gave me errands to run and gave me tips that I faithfully saved to take home with me. By the end of the three months I had saved up 120 Austrian schillings, enough to buy a used sled to use during the long winters. We now had warm coats to wear. It took half an hour to walk up the hill to the local school. We walked on top of the frozen snow. I would open my coat to shield the children behind me from the icy winds.

School was mandatory through the eighth grade. We also went to school on Saturdays to be able to complete our education. It was the equivalent of high school. At the age of fourteen you either went on to higher education, if you could afford it, or as most of us had to do, become apprentices for three years to learn a trade. My sister Lydia learned to become a beautician, and I wanted to become a seamstress. However, there was no place available, so many girls had applied. So, I became an apprentice in a grocery store and had to attend business school one day a week.

The conditions in the camp had improved. We were allowed to make a vegetable garden and even have some chickens. We lived all summer from the produce. Mom made a root cellar by digging a hole in the ground to store potatoes, cabbage and carrots for the winter. She covered it with straw and dirt. One time we received a "care" package with a wonderful bar of American cheese, milk powder and egg powder, etc. Every other Sunday we had a meal from one chicken for a family of eight. I remember eating the feet (claws) of that chicken and still love to nibble on the bones.

The barracks still had no insulation. We used a bucket to carry water from a well in the center of our camp, about a city block away. When winter came a plumber had to thaw out the pump so we could get water. Back in the kitchen, a thin sheet of ice usually formed on the bucket of water. The barracks with toilets were next to the well. They were pit toilets and you had to stand up and aim. For toilet paper we used broad leaves of grass when available.

Someone invented a stove fired by sawdust. An oil drum was used with a beam in the center, packed down with sawdust all around tightly, so that when the beam was removed the air could circulate when it was lit. The fire would heat up the drum glowing red hot. I'm still amazed that we did not have any fires in those barracks. At night before going to bed we would hover around that stove to warm up our feather coverlets and rush into bed. The twin beds were too narrow for our growing bodies, so we slept one at the foot of the bed and the other one at the head, smelling each other's feet.

Mondays were washdays. We carried wash water in buckets from the well, and then had to heat it on the stove. White wash was boiled and all the wash was scrubbed on a washboard. There was a competition among the women, who had the whitest laundry on the lines. I remember when my mother had a bicycle accident and was laid up. I had to take my turn in doing the laundry, and Mom would inspect every piece. If it was not clean enough to her liking, it went back onto the scrubbing board. The knuckles on my fingers were bleeding from all the scrubbing.

As I mentioned before, I was born into a fundamental Christian family, but we had no church in the camp. So, all the born again Christians gathered together and worshipped as best we could. As time passed, we were ministered to by a church in Salzburg. The church was in the American Zone and supported by the Americans. Every other week a pastor or lay pastor would come by train and hold services for us. We put aside one of our rooms for them to be able to stay for the weekend. A barracks was assigned for us to hold church services in, and a pump organ was donated that my mom played on. One of my most precious memories is of my mom gathering us children to sing together in three-part harmony.

When a young couple from Philadelphia came on a mission trip to Salzburg, Austria, they developed a plan to hold evangelistic meetings in the city of Villach, five kilometers from our camp. The pastor of the church in Salzburg by the name of Martin Gigelseder was the evangelist. My sister Lydia was allowed to attend with the adults on the first night of the meetings. I had to stay home and babysit my younger sisters. I cried my heart out for I wanted to go. The Lord had prepared my almost thirteen-year-old heart for the need of the Savior.

I had a dream that the refugee camp was totally empty of people. I looked up into the sky and saw all kinds of signs that made me think that the end of the world was at hand. I screamed and asked the Lord to please not let that happen, because I was not saved yet. I was allowed to attend the meeting the next day, and Lydia had to stay home with our younger sisters. When the invitation was given to receive Christ as Savior, my hand flew up and I went forward. I knew that I was a sinner but was afraid that God would not want me for I was so bad. I had a vicious temper and fought with my sisters even to pulling hair. You could attribute this to the horrible living condition and the trauma we went through, but I took full responsibility for my behavior.

The lyrics of the invitation song was an encouragement to me, for in the refrain it said, "*Jesus will save you now, if your sins are as red as scarlet He will make you white as snow.*" I went forward with tears streaming down my face. I prayed to receive God's forgiveness because Jesus took the punishment that I deserved when He died on the cross. On the third day He rose again, and I had a living Savior. A burden was lifted off me and a joy filled my heart when I accepted His salvation.

With my childish understanding I believed that from now on I would never lose my temper, or sin again. The first time I lost my temper, I just wanted to die and go to heaven. I did not know that daily cleansing was available:

1.John 1:9 *"If I confess my sin, He is faithful and just to forgive my sin and cleanse me from all unrighteousness."*

I did not even own a Bible. On my thirteenth birthday I received a used Bible. I could not get enough of reading God's word, but I also needed help with understanding it.

The periodic visits from a pastor, really were not enough to allow me to grow spiritually. One of the lay preachers by the name of Willy Friedsam, also a refugee, was assigned by the church in Salzburg to come to minister to us every other week. Before I could get baptized by immersion I had to prove myself for one year that my conversion was real. Then I was baptized.

Chapter Seven
America!

Willy Friedsam, Onkel Willy as we called him, was going to America, where his brother-in-law lived in Iowa. He was able to find a sponsor for himself and his wife. When they arrived at the Idlewild Airport, the pastor of the German Baptist church met them, and took them to the Grand Central Station where they took a train to Iowa.

Onkel Willy told that pastor of our desire to immigrate, and that we needed a sponsor. He gave our address to the pastor, who in turn started corresponding with my mother. It took a whole year before we were cleared to immigrate. The requirements to have a clean background and excellent health, were very strict. I did not pass the health inspection, for it was found that I still had a shadow on my lungs from the pneumonia when I was six years old.

I had to go for x-rays every month for a whole year, to make sure that I did not have tuberculosis. The sponsor had to guarantee a place for us to live, and work, so we would not become a burden to the government

With only a few weeks to go, there still was no place found for us to live. With much prayer the searching went on. Then the pastor's wife saw a "for rent" sign on a storefront window. She went across the street to the used car lot and spoke to the owner of the building who was willing to rent it to us for $60.00 a month. We also had to pay for the heating. She restrained herself from hugging that man, and told us that she nearly kissed a Jew for the joy of renting the place to us.

The Immanuel Baptist Church in New York City met the requirements, for they had sponsored hundreds of refugees. The pastor was able to secure the money from the World Council of Churches to pay our fare on either ship or plane, with the requirement that it had to be paid back as soon as possible

Now all was ready for us. We left the Munich airport in Germany on a four-propeller airplane that took 26 Hours with two stops for refueling, and arrived in New York's Idlewild airport.

We entered the promised land, the United States of America, on September 26, 1956.

The Pastor and another man came with two cars to pick us up. I do not remember seeing the Statue of Liberty at the gateway to America in the New York harbor. We did not have to go through Ellis Island where previously all immigrants had to enter. It was closed and not used any longer. Arriving at our storefront apartment, we marveled at the generosity of the church

The church members had cleaned the place and put used furniture in. We agreed to give it back for the next immigrants when we were able to get our own. Later we helped clean the apartment and get it ready for the next influx of immigrants.

I will never forget seeing our pastor in his late fifties as he carried a refrigerator on his back, up a narrow five flights of stairs. Two young people brought up the rear assisting him.

The women of the missionary society filled the refrigerator with so much food, including a big chunk of bologna and all necessary food that we needed to get us started.

We couldn't believe our eyes when we saw the full refrigerator and the big ten-pound bag of potatoes. Even onions and garlic, were provided.

One of the deacons and his wife came with a gallon of ice cream to welcome us. We were now in America the promised "Land of the Free."

Our storefront apartment was in Queens, very near the LaGuardia Airport, and the planes came very close over our heads. The noise was something we had to get used to, for during the occupation in Austria there was no air traffic.

One day I had to get to the grocery store to buy "Gries," I did not know the English word for it and asked if any one spoke German. The store manager was a Jew, and their Yiddish language was close to German. He went on the phone to call his mom. When she answered he put the phone to my ear so I could tell her what I needed. She said it was cream of wheat.

Because of the holocaust, Germans were hated, but those people were very kind to me.

We couldn't wait to become citizens of this wonderful land, being so grateful for the opportunity to live, work, and partake of all the blessings this land affords. When the five-year waiting period was up, we proudly swore our allegiance to the United States of America and became citizens.

Chapter Eight
Our New Church

Freedom to worship, at last! The best thing for me was the church services. On the first Sunday after our arrival, at the beginning of the Sunday School everyone who had a birthday that week went forward and put coins into a little bank. A little African child nodded his head when the coins were put in. My sixteenth birthday was three days before, but I did not have sixteen coins. Someone graciously gave them to me. As I put them in one at a time, everyone counted my years.

Having a Sunday School, with beautiful Bible story pictures to take home, was exciting to me, and I just wanted to collect them and send them home to Austria. After a few months I was allowed to teach a second-grade class in German.

We joined the choir that was led by our pastor. We also joined a youth group, also led by our pastor. His preaching was so wonderful, and I soaked it up like a dry sponge. Here was spiritual food for me to grow on.

One of my favorite Bible stories is from Luke 10:39, where Mary of Bethany was found seated at Jesus feet and listened to every word Jesus spoke. Jesus said that she had chosen the better part. I just wanted to be like Mary.

Wednesday nights were for our prayer meetings and Bible study, and Friday nights for our choir practice. The morning service was in German and the choir also sang in German. But the evening service was in English. Our pastor, we called him Onkel Hussmann, spoke a very precise English, slowly so that we were able to learn quickly. It never occurred to us that the people here had to learn German because we did not speak English. We gladly learned English, the language of the land.

Chapter Nine
In the Work Force

I should have gone to high school at sixteen, but being the second oldest of six children, (My mom had remarried and had two more girls.) my sister Lydia and I had to go to work to get the family established and help pay back the money for our passage.

My parents, Lydia and I all needed jobs. Our pastor went with me to get a work permit since I was not yet seventeen. Then he went with us to help us search for a job.

Our pastor's wife told me that I had to change my hairstyle, for with my long braids I looked like a twelve-year old. So, I pulled my long hair into a bun at the nape of my neck and looked older like a babushka. Our pastor checked the newspaper daily for any job offers.

When he found one for me, he took me to a factory. At the initial interview I was refused because I did not speak English. My pastor persisted, asking if there was any one there who spoke German. A young woman in another department was found, and I was introduced to the boss lady, who took one look at me and assured my pastor that she would be like a mother to me. I got the job.

The young woman who spoke a little German had come to America from Germany when she was three years old and had forgotten much of her mother tongue. She made a deal with me that if I would teach her German, she would teach me English.

I gladly went to work, but I had only one dress for work to wear. The same dress was washed on Saturday to get it ready for the following week. The assistant to my boss came to work every day with a different outfit on. She asked our boss lady if I would be insulted if she brought me some of her hand-me-downs. I had told them that I had five sisters at home, and so she brought me two large bags full of beautiful clothes to share with my sisters. I made $1.00 an hour and gave my Mom $20.00 each week. I also repaid for my fare to the United States. After my tithe and subway tokens to go to work, there was nothing left.

My family could not afford the rent and heating bills. We found a "Super job" with free rent in return for washing down the hallways, and keeping the coal furnace in the basement fed. We had to carry buckets of water up five flights of stairs and wash all the hallways on every floor.

One day as I arrived home from work, my mom left for the second shift, leaving me in charge of my younger sisters. A fight broke out between two of them. Normally I would have lost my temper and beaten both of them up. This time however I just folded my hands and prayed. It became very quiet and I realized the power of prayer, for I did not lose my temper and would have felt guilty. I had a great sense of victory and was praising the Lord. I was growing in the Lord! This was a valuable lesson that I could draw on when the need arrived.

In preparation for a Billy Graham crusade in 1957, many extra prayer meetings were held during the week in churches and in private homes. Then in May the crusade started in the old Madison Square Garden. There was so much response, it was extended twice into the beginning of September, but I never tired of the meetings. We sang in the 3000-voice choir every night. My girlfriend from our church, who sat next to me in the choir, told me the scripture passages that Billy Graham used to preach from. I read them in my German Bible to follow along. To see the thousands of peoples come forward during the invitation to receive Christ as their Savior every night, still gives me "glory bumps".

Chapter Ten
Oskar

Four months after our arrival in America, the Lehotsky family came from Germany. They too were refugees from Yugoslavia. After the war ended, they wanted to go home where the father had a blacksmith shop. Just before they were to leave Germany for Yugoslavia one of their five children, a nine-year-old boy named Oskar found an unexploded shell. Curious to see what was in it, he used a rock to open it. It exploded injuring Oskar next to his eye and at the side of his knee. He carried those scars for the rest of his life.

An American soldier, who was having his lunch outside, saw it, dropped his tray and raced him to the hospital. The Lord used the incident to prevent them from returning to Yugoslavia. The family missed the transport that would have taken them home. That saved their lives for they would have been captured and put into a concentration camp. They stayed in Germany and were fortunate to be in the American zone.

The Lehotsky family immigrated to America with their two youngest sons on an old troop transport ship, the *USS General Harry Tailor*. The winter storms over the Atlantic Ocean nearly did them in. The ship was on its last voyage and almost did not make it. It was later scrapped at the Brooklyn Navy Yard. They could have come on a plane, but the father was afraid of flying.

I wonder if he regretted his decision for they had to wear life jackets the whole time and were seasick most of the trip. It was February of 1957 when they arrived in New York's Brooklyn Navy Yard. Oskar had his trade from Germany and found a job at a German owned place as a tool and die maker. He was paid only $1.25 per hour when others in his trade received $5.00 an hour. After a while he asked for a raise and was told that he did not speak English and was lucky to have a job. Oskar took the tool he was working on and asked if that tool knew that. He shamed his boss in to giving him a five-cent raise.

Working a 50-hour week, he brought home $65.00 and gave his mother $50.00. He also paid for the whole family's trip to America. His mother used only $15.00 a week for groceries for a family of four, and they had a "Super job" with free rent. They saved enough money to buy their own house six years later.

The family attended our German Immanuel Baptist Church. Oskar and I met in church. We both attended the youth group, and sang in our choir. We also both sang with the Billy Graham 3,000 voice choir at the crusade in the old Madison Square Garden. Each night after the meeting he would escort me home on the New York subway. That was the beginning of our dating. Oskar accepted the Lord as his savior about a month after the Billy Graham Crusade.

His parents did not like me, for they had someone younger in mind. We wanted to get married, but because he was not yet twenty-one, he needed parental approval, and they refused. They did not want to lose the income from him. So, we had to wait.

We got engaged on October 4, 1958, and started our search for an apartment that we could afford. My parents managed an 86-family house on the outskirts of the Bronx, and the Lehotskys had a similar job in a bad section of the Bronx. An apartment became available in their building, but we did not want to live near either one of the families to avoid jealousy.

We continued to look in all five boroughs of New York City. It was getting close to our wedding day and we still had not found a place to live that we could afford.

At the beginning of January, the landlord of the 86 family-house my parents managed, came to pick up the rent monies and almost stepped into a pile of dog dung on the marble floor of the entrance foyer. He asked if this happened often and was told "yes." He was a Jewish lawyer. He sent letters to each of the dog owners to either get rid of their dogs or vacate their apartments.

An elderly couple lived on the fifth floor with their little dog. They were childless and considered their dog like family. They had lived in that apartment for 25 years and paid only $25.00 a month rent. Because of rent control the landlord could not raise the rent. In order not to lose their dog, they chose to move out and pay a much higher rent somewhere else.

That apartment became available, and we took it as a gift from the Lord. The apartment was renovated, painted, and given a new refrigerator and stove to justify raising the rent. We ended up paying $57.00 a month, heat and water included. All other apartments that we looked at asked for $80.00 and more. My in-laws were angry because we chose to turn down the apartment in their place and vowed never to set foot in our place.

The apartment in the house where they lived was a railroad apartment with a window on one end. You had to walk from one end through the bedrooms that had no windows to the living room that had the other window. Ours was a beautiful apartment with big rooms. The bedroom had two windows and was big enough for a baby's crib, once we had one. The living room was big enough for a dining room set on one side. The eat-in kitchen was small but cozy. There was a large walk-in closet in the foyer.

Oskar had given me a choice, either an engagement diamond ring, or a bedroom set when we were engaged. I decided that we could not sleep on a diamond ring. We bought our bed room set and had enough for a sofa for the living room.

We did not want to start out with debts, so we only bought when we had saved enough money to pay cash. We first bought a radio with a record player for the living room, then a few months later we bought a television set. One day on the way to the subway to go to church, we saw a nice dining room set in the window of a furniture store. It cost only $350.00, for a man had put a down payment on it, but was drafted and could not buy it. We had saved enough money to be able to afford it. I still have that set today.

The wedding was set for February 4, 1959. three weeks after Oskar's 21st birthday. We were married at our church. The wedding had to go according to Oskar's parents' wishes. I would have loved to have had the wedding march played, but they insisted on a hymn, and we had to walk down the aisle together. Our pastor tried to intervene, but they said if we did not follow their orders that they would not attend. I had never seen our pastor so angry, but he could not change their minds, so we relented to keep the peace.

My mother-in-law tried to tell me that I had to live on a weekly budget of $7.50 for she only needed $15.00 for a family of four. My husband stood up to her and said that we will manage our own budget. He wanted more than two slices of white bread with one slice of American cheese for his lunch like he and his father received every day. Money never became an issue in all of our 53 and a half years of marriage, for we held each other accountable, and I kept a strict record of our spending.

My mom told us that marriage was like a diamond in the rough. The more the rough edges were polished off the more beautiful it becomes. The Lord did a lot of polishing for we were so young. The Lord took my mother home to heaven on January 9,1961, one day before her 42nd birthday. She died of kidney failure before there was any dialysis available.

My stepfather threw out all the pictures my Mom had brought out from Yugoslavia. One day when I went to the trash cans in the basement to discard my trash, I miraculously found the pictures. There was a row of twelve trashcans. For some reason, I picked up the lid of the third one and I saw the pictures lying on top of the trash. Undoubtedly the Lord led me to the right one to preserve them for me. If someone had put their trash on top of them, they would have been lost to me forever. Pictures of my father were among them. God was at work again!

We postponed our honeymoon till spring, for we wanted to tour our nation's capital by walking to all the sights. We did not own a car. The next day after the wedding, one of our deacons came to our door to take us to church in his car, to make sure that we would come to church. We already had left to use the subway. It was our goal to start our married life by attending church regularly.

Oskar and a coworker, Hans Jungsberger, wanted to start their own business as partners. Hans quit his job to go find clients after they set up shop. Oskar gave half of his salary to his partner to live on until they got some contracts. Oskar would work ten hours at his job and then go to his business and work there to fill the incoming orders. Sometimes he would sleep on the subway. They started the business without any debts, and were doing well.

When the German boss found out what the two men were doing, he got mad. He retaliated by firing Oskar, and because he was on the draft board, he got Oskar drafted into the Army. The result was that Oskar lost his part of the business. His partner had just landed a $30,000.00 contract which was huge in those days.

Hans promised Oskar that he would welcome him back as a partner when he finished his tour of duty, but when that time came, he refused to honor his promise.

In retrospect, despite losing the partnership, God turned it into a blessing. Oskar found a job in New Jersey, and we were able to leave New York.

Chapter Eleven
Oskar and the Army

Oskar had to report for duty within three weeks. Before coming to America, Oskar had to sign an agreement to serve in the military for two years. He was happy to do so, being grateful to be allowed in this country, but the timing was just unfortunate.

We were married for three years and did not have any children yet. This was our first separation from each other. He served in Fort Dix, New Jersey, only 60 miles from home. It was during the Vietnam war. After basic training the troops were deployed to different parts of the country or overseas. The word got out that only a few men were to stay in Fort Dix. I prayed that Oskar might be one of them.

Oskar wanted to go to Germany to be an interpreter, for he spoke fluent German. I would have been allowed to go with him. He however was chosen to stay in Fort Dix to become a teacher of communication, teaching Morse code. That enabled him to come home on certain weekends. On our seventh anniversary Oskar gave me a diamond ring.

I worked for the Burroughs Welcome Pharmaceutical Company until I became pregnant. They had a policy that pregnant women could not work in the same building that did research with radioactive materials. For that reason I was laid off. I was denied unemployment and searched for work every day, but no one would give me a job because I was pregnant. I paid the rent, gas and electricity, and had $15.00 a month left to live on. Thank God for the low rent.

The Lord blessed us with a beautiful baby girl in January of 1965, just two months before Oskar's discharge from the

Army. My mother-in-law mocked me because it was *only* a girl, and that I was only capable of having girls since I came from a family of six girls. She forgot that her own daughter in Germany had only three girls and no boys.

When Oskar's tour of duty was completed in March of 1965, he had to find a job. He still served in the army reserve until February of 1969. We wanted to get out of New York and into the country for fresh air and sunshine. As nice as our apartment was, we still had to battle the soot from the chimneys. When I went to the flat roof to hang out the diapers and laundry, I put my baby girl into a basket for I never left her alone in the apartment. Within minutes she was covered with soot even into her eyeballs. I was so upset, for I took pride, keeping my baby immaculately clean.

Chapter Twelve
Leaving the City

We just wanted to get out of the city into the country where there was clean fresh air. Oskar found a job in Dover, New Jersey as a tool and mold maker, and we were able to move.

My In-laws had bought a small house on a lake not too far from Oskar's job, and they rented it to us, for they were not ready to retire. It cost us much more than we paid for our beautiful big apartment in New York, but we were in the country.

They came every weekend to *their* house, even though we paid rent. I had my little girl in the playpen set up outside all day weather permitting, while I made a vegetable garden and mowed the lawn. I was told by the pediatrician that she was "a picture of health."

When Dorothy was eleven months old, I had a miscarriage. Before Oskar was able to get home from work, I could only lay down on the sofa with my little girl in the playpen in front of me. She started to cry and I could not even pick her up. So, I prayed, "Lord, please take over." She laid down and went to sleep until her daddy came home. I realized if I started to hemorrhage, I could be dead before help arrived. Looking around at my sleeping baby, I committed my husband and baby to the Lord, knowing that He would take care of them.

A supernatural peace enveloped me. I had no fear of dying. All I could think of was the song, *"Lord I'm coming home."* But the Lord had other plans for me. We did not even have a doctor yet. I called the Christian radio station to ask for the name of a doctor. I was referred to a gynecologist that the owner's wife went to. The gynecologist said that it was a complete miscarriage. I did not even have to have a scraping or go to the hospital. Thank you, Lord! We were new in the area, and I had no one to take care of my baby girl.

Two years later the Lord blessed us with a baby boy. Our Johnny was born on January 13, 1967.

Oskar was working hard on a project that the engineers had developed, but it was not proven yet. The project took six months, and Oskar worried that it might not succeed. Subconsciously, he took the job home, as a result he developed an ulcer. The doctor suggested that he get another job.

An opportunity came for him to work for M&M Mars in Hackettstown, New Jersey as a maintenance mechanic with less worry and much more pay. He took that job, although it was a five-day swing shift. We called it the *mad* shift, midnight, afternoon, and day, with a five-day rotation. Living literally by the calendar was not easy, for there was no Monday to Friday week. Oskar advanced to stationary engineer in the sewer plant, then in the power plant.

We saved our money to be able to buy our own house. One became available only one mile from the plant. It was a ranch house with three bedrooms, living room, dining room, and one and a half bathrooms. It was T shaped. In the front was the garage. In the middle was the kitchen, and to the back, a big room was added for a family room. It was perfect, for the master bedroom faced the front of the house, and the children were able to play in the family room to the rear. They still had to play quietly when Daddy was sleeping.

To get the mortgage approved we needed just $50.00 more for the down payment. Our German neighbors loaned it to us, for Oskar's parents refused it. We moved on January 11,

1968, with our three-year-old girl and one-year-old boy. It was a development with lots of children. As we drove up the street, our three-year-old little girl cried out in excitement, "Schau Mami, KINDER! (Look there are children here!)" Where we had lived, there were no children, unless people came there for vacation or on weekends.

One day when Dorothy was just two, I had to go with her into the city seven miles away. We saw an African-American mother with her small child. Dorothy had never seen a black child before. She yelled out, "Ist der schmutzig?" (Is he dirty?) I was so glad she said it in German. I reminded her of the children's song, "*Jesus loves the little children, red and yellow, black and white, they are precious in His sight.*"

Oskar had to sleep during the day two out of every three weeks. I had the job of keeping the children quiet, for Oskar was a light sleeper. My three-year-old and one-year-old were less of a problem than the neighbor's children. At the end of the five days my nerves were raw. I would mow the lawn when he was at work, and in the winter, I got up early to shovel the driveway before he came home from the night shift at 7am.

When the children were at school, I took a part time job at the local deli, with the understanding that on Oskar's day off, or when the children were home from school, I would not work. My boss was very understanding. He, his wife and I worked together like family. I also did some alterations for the local cleaner and worked at home for my own customers around Oskar's schedule. This way I contributed to the family budget. My priority was to be a good wife and stay-at-home mother. Every week on Oskar's day off, we went on a date, went bowling or out to lunch.

The company started a new work schedule that included a weekend shift of four twelve-hour days. The pay would have been more, and it would have been steady daytime. It was very tempting, but that would mean no church attendance for him. With the swing shift he was able to attend the morning service one week, and the evening service the alternate week. I did not want to influence him in the decision, but just prayed and asked the Lord to guide him. He declined the offer to take the day shift. He told me that he would be a bad example to his children by putting work ahead of the Lord. That spoke volumes to me, and he grew to be ten feet tall in my eyes.

Chapter Thirteen
Vacation Camping

Every year we used Oskar's two-week vacation to go camping. Our pastor loaned us his tent, and all necessary equipment to try out camping before we invested in a tent of our own. Oskar was used to camping for he was a boy scout in Germany, but I had never gone camping before. It was an affordable way to go on vacation and see the country.

I remember our first camping trip to Lake George in New York state. The state park had only pit toilets, but there were coin operated showers available. One afternoon while sitting in an ice arena, watching the athletes practice for the winter Olympics in Lake Placid, we heard a heavy rainstorm pelting the tin roof of the building. When we returned to our camp, we found that the floor of our tent was not waterproof. We had to sleep in the back of our Volkswagen station wagon. We knew enough not to touch the walls of the tent when it rained.

I did enjoy camping for it was a complete break-away from our daily routine and gave us an opportunity to go sight-seeing. Oskar was the cook, and the rest of us did the clean-up. The children enjoyed gathering sticks for the camp fire.

The next year we bought a Sears tent with a waterproof floor, and a cook stove, and we were ready to go camping. We chose to go to Algonquin Park in Ontario, Canada. Under a sunny sky we drove through nice rolling hills and reached our destination in the evening. After setting up camp, we soon had the children snuggled up in sleeping bags. Then, Oskar and I enjoyed a romantic setting under a starlit sky around a campfire.

Our four-year old son Johnny had a bad habit of sucking his thumb. Nothing we said or threatened would convince him to quit. For months every time Johnny saw a puppy, he would beg for one. Finally, while on this trip, Oskar promised him that if he would quit sucking his thumb, he would get his puppy. It worked. That night in the tent, he stuck his hands under the pillow to keep his thumb from going to his mouth. He was committed, and he got his puppy, a beagle.

During the night however, it started to rain. The temperature dropped to where we were able to see our breath when we talked. We brought the cook stove inside and had our meals in the tent. After three days of rain and cold we just packed up our wet tent and drove south to the Thousand Islands, where we set up camp on a sunny spot to dry out our tent. The temperature was rising up to close to 100 degrees. We were not able to go into the tent because of the heat, even though we opened all the windows.

Next to our campsite was a family with eight children. They had bunk beds in the tent, and some of them slept in their boat. We saw that they also had a screen house set up over the picnic tables. That inspired us to buy one also, as well as a heater. The father asked Oskar if he would be willing to drive the boat, so they could water-ski. We were delighted to go on a boat ride for the first time in our lives.

Some of our camping trips took us down to Virginia. We chose the last week in August, right before Labor Day and just before our children started school. South of the border of Pennsylvania, school started already in mid-August, so the campgrounds were less crowded.

Our camp was in the center of Virginia, and we took daily trips to the surrounding areas. We learned some of the history of our new homeland by visiting Monticello, the home of Thomas Jefferson, third President of our country. He was the author of the Declaration of Independence and the Statutes of Virginia, and was a strong advocate for religious freedom.

Virginia was considered the "cradle of presidents," for eight of our presidents were born there. We were not far from the Skyline Drive which leads into the Blue Ridge Parkway.

On our trips we learned the names of the different states with their capitals. So, our children were well informed with information when they returned back to school and had to write a report of their summer.

When Oskar received three weeks of vacation, we were able to go all the way west to Yellowstone Park. What a wonderful experience to see the geysers, and watch Old Faithful erupt right on schedule. We saw many animals like bear, buffalo, elk, mule deer, and many more.

Climbing up Mount Washborn in Yellowstone was an experience I'll never forget. The view from the top was breathtaking. Unlike the Alps of Austria, the Rocky Mountains. are higher and spread far apart. There were some wildflowers like we had in Austria that I loved so much and missed in New Jersey.

We went south to Salt Lake City, Utah and the North Rim of the Grand Canyon. We were unable to take the mule ride down because they were booked one year in advance. Besides, our Johnny was too small. Disappointed, we were on the way back to camp, when we passed a small airfield that offered plane rides over the Grand Canyon, what an experience that was!

On Sundays we always found a gospel preaching church, and it was wonderful to worship with like-minded believers even on our vacation.

Chapter Fourteen
Children Grow Up

After graduating from high school, our daughter Dorothy attended Messiah College in Pennsylvania. After four years at that Christian college, she graduated and found work as a health inspector for the Dover Health Department. Through a friend in our church who was also an alumnus of Messiah College, she was introduced to a Christian young man who had also gone to Messiah College. Philip Peterson called himself a Connecticut Yankee.

He and Dorothy had never met in school. He was in his senior year when Dorothy was a freshman. She was studying nursing, and Philip was an accountant. One year after they were introduced, they were married, on November 16, 1991. She moved to Connecticut to Philip's hometown. On May 21, 1994 they presented us with Daniel, our first grandchild. Then on March 7, 1996, our Stephanie came along, and on March 26, 1998, Mary Elisabeth was born.

Daniel is now attending Liberty University in Lynchburg, Virginia. Stephanie has graduated from Clark Summit Baptist University.

After we moved to Georgia, our son John met and married a wonderful Christian girl, Lisa, on November 14, 2003. She already had an eight-year old son, Craig, from her first marriage. They were married on the beach in Jamaica. Craig walked his mother down the hotel steps to the gazebo over the water where the ceremony took place.

My sisters and I, and my daughter Dorothy, sang, "O glorious Love." The pastor who performed the ceremony asked us to stay and sing at his church, but we had to get home.

Johnny and Lisa, with Craig, moved to Cashiers, North Carolina where he built a successful construction business. On September 20, 2007, they presented us with our fifth grandchild, a perfect little boy, Samuel. We called him Sammy.

Chapter Fifteen
Retirement

My in-laws moved to Florida after Oskar's father retired. From then on, our vacations were spent with them in Florida. Three of my five sisters also moved to Florida, about three hours south of the Lehotskys in Boca Raton, and we were able to visit them as well.

Oskar got tired of Florida, and in 1983 we made plans with my sister Lydia and her husband Eberhard to meet in Georgia. They knew of a town in the Georgia mountains named Helen that looked like a Bavarian village. We made plans to meet there in October when the colors were at their peak. We forgot about the Oktoberfest and made no reservations.

The night before we were to leave New Jersey, they called to tell us not to come. They had been told that there was no room to be found within 100 miles radius of Helen.

Lydia and Eberhard drove north to Hiawassee where they hoped to find a German acquaintance. It was on a Sunday morning when they arrived at the Georgia Mountain Restaurant for breakfast. They asked the hostess to direct them to a gospel preaching church they could attend. She sent them to McConnell Memorial Baptist Church.

The usher that morning was Gene Brumbaugh, a real estate agent. He and his wife took them out on Lake Chatuge to show them the beautiful area. Henrietta Brumbaugh also handled rentals. Arrangements were made for all of us to come the next May. That was how the Lord brought us to Hiawassee, Georgia.

We fell in love with the area, and decided to vacation in Hiawassee the following year. On our walks we saw a cabin with a "for rent or sale" sign. We were observed looking around by the owner on top of the hill. She came down and showed us the one-bedroom cabin. She said that the contract with the real estate agent would expire in October, and that she would sell it to us more reasonably after that.

We decided that it was cheaper to buy than to rent, so in October we came down from New Jersey to buy that cabin. Oskar still was not ready to retire, but we had wonderful vacations here in the Georgia mountains. We attended McConnell Memorial Baptist Church and felt blessed every time we came. Greeted with *"welcome home"* every time, it became evident that the Lord was leading us here.

We started to look for property to build our house on. Gene Brumbaugh knew of property that was for sale, but had not even been listed yet. The property had much more acreage than we were looking for, but the owner was not willing to divide the twenty-four acres. When we prayed about it and saw the location with a beautiful view, we knew it was meant for us. The seller Willy Sprinkles was willing to hold the mortgage for two years at ten percent interest.

After 26 and half years of working the swing shift at M&M Mars, Oskar was able to take an early retirement at the age of 56. The last few years he had worked many twelve-hour shifts, and with overtime he built up a nice pension.

That enabled us to sell our house, move to Georgia and begin building our retirement house. It was hard to leave our daughter and her family and move so far away, but the real estate taxes in New Jersey were too high to afford in retirement. At least twice a year we drove the nearly 1000 miles to Connecticut to visit, and they also came down to Georgia on vacation. We alternated Christmas visits with each other.

Northeast Georgia still had four distinct seasons, but not the long severe winters like up north. The beauty of the area reminded me of Austria. I also had two sisters living here and we were able to worship together in the same church, sing in the choir, and also sing as the "Star Sisters Trio."

It had been Oskar's dream to build his own house. With help from our son John, the process began in 1994. It still amazes me that my husband, the "tool and die maker" had the courage to do all the electric, plumbing, wood floors and tiles by himself. He was used to "zero tolerance" and worked very precisely. Many times, I joked and said, "Oskar, please throw away your micrometer. You are working with wood now, not metal." But for him, everything had to be precisely accurate. His widowed mom would call from Florida, and we had to drop everything and drive down to fix whatever she needed. It took five years to complete the house.

We brought his mom up to Hiawassee to see if she liked it. She too fell in love with the area and liked our church. So, she sold her house in Florida, and we moved her up here. We lived in that one-bedroom cabin while we built our house. Mom got the bed room, Oskar slept in the recliner, and I slept on the floor on cushions.

We built Mom her own apartment in our house, at ground level so she did not need to climb stairs. She had her own kitchen, dining room, and living room, a bathroom with a seat in the shower, and a bedroom with a very large walk-in closet. Sadly, she was only able to enjoy it for one and a half years. She died of liver cancer.

I treasure the memory of when we were able to take Oskar's mom on a trip through Germany and Austria the year after her husband died in 1984. She still had a daughter with family and a son living in Germany. She loved to travel.

Finally, our home was completed, and with both children settled in their own homes, we were able to travel.

Chapter Sixteen
Greece

Our camping trip to Greece began on May 15, 2001. On a trip to Germany and Austria where I still had relatives, my Aunt and Uncle invited us to go camping with them on a trip to Greece. They had a camper which we took with us on a large ship that departed from Venice, Italy.

It was very interesting to watch the boarding of tractor-trailers on the lower deck, then campers, cars, and motorcycles on the next deck. Each deck had washrooms with toilets and showers. We were able to sleep in our camper, other passengers just found an unoccupied space on the floor, sleeping in their sleeping bags. The top floors were like a five-star hotel, with beautiful dining rooms with mirrored walls. The food was excellent.

We camped for five weeks, touring many ancient sites in Athens, ancient Corinth, Olympia, and the southernmost tip of the European continent. In Athens, we stood on top of the Acropolis with its Parthenon, looking around to see Mars Hill. On the way down I stopped at a souvenir place and asked the attendant where Mars Hill was. She pointed downhill.

I wanted to see the place where the apostle Paul was conversing with the philosophers, as recorded in the Bible in Acts 17:16-32. They took him to the Areopagus. When he saw an altar to the unknown God, he proclaimed to them the God of heaven and the world and everything in it. He gave them the gospel. Sadly, we did not see any evidence of Christianity. Yes, there were lots of ornate Greek Orthodox churches, but they were mostly like museums. There was much of history and many ruins of temples to their gods.

As we camped outside of ancient Corinth, we toured the old city ruins. I searched for any sign of the Agora where the apostle Paul spent eighteen months proclaiming the gospel. We could not find it, though we heard that there was a small plaque that marked the place.

My heart was heavy, until I followed a group of tourists from England that were following the missionary journey of the apostle Paul. They had come from Ephesus in Turkey, over to Thessalonika, down to Athens, and now to Corinth. How I praised the Lord for the timing of meeting that group. They had stopped at that little sign that we missed, and had a worship service.

Afterwards, we climbed to the top of Acrocorintos with a good view of Corinth by the Sea. We continued on over a high mountain with many hairpin turns. Amazingly, tractor-trailers used those roads to get to the other side. We saw a highway with many tunnels through the mountains being built with the funding of the European Union. This will be a great help for the traffic.

Our next campsite was at the foot of Meteora. That is one of the largest and most important complexes of Greek Orthodox monasteries. In a region of almost inaccessible sandstone peaks, Monks had settled and built unbelievable monasteries. Today they can be visited by car, but in ancient times the Monks had to be lowered by ropes in a basket.

These are just a few highlights of our trip to Greece.

As we traveled back on the ship north, we saw Italy to the west and the Albanian and Croatian coastline on the east. We passed Bosnia-Herzegovina. Standing on the top of the ship watching a beautiful sunset, I asked my uncle if I would ever be able to set foot again in the land of my birth. That set a plan in motion for us to come back the following year and go camping to Croatia.

Chapter Seventeen
Croatia

On May 16, 2002, we flew over the Atlantic Ocean to Austria and prepared for our camping trip to Croatia. It was the first time in 58 years that I would set foot in the land of my birth. My aunt had planned a great itinerary. She would have made an excellent travel agent.

We made our way south along the Adriatic Sea, staying at very nice campgrounds with tiled bathrooms, bathrooms that had Kimberly Clark hand towels and bathroom tissues. The campgrounds had rooms with stainless steel sinks to wash dishes, washing machines and ironing boards, all very modern and clean. I actually took pictures, for I did not expect that in Croatia.

My aunt and uncle, Ricki and Viktor Gasteiger, have camped there many times, yet they marveled at the modern improvements of the roads. They were paved where before they were gravel.

Most of the cities were still surrounded by walls, erected hundreds of years earlier to protect the residents. We saw many harbors with sail boats along the way.

Our most southern campground was just outside of Dubrovnik. My aunt and uncle had camped with their family there many times before the war of 1991. Dubrovnik is called the Pearl of the Adria. Many cruise ships anchor outside in deep waters, and bring tourists into the harbor on tender boats.

Entering the city through large gates, we were able to walk on top of the walls and look down into the ancient city. I

asked my uncle why so many roofs had new red tiles. He said it
was because of the war of 1991. When the city was shelled, the
old roofs were damaged, but thankfully the houses had not been
completely destroyed. There is so much history dating back to
the 7th century. Europe's oldest pharmacy is in Dubrovnik.

The condition of our campground however broke my aunt
and uncle's heart. The once beautiful campground was only half
restored after the destruction of the war. The five-star hotel next
to the campground was in shambles, never restored to its former
beauty.

We spent four weeks touring Croatia. Our last camping
stop was outside of Zagreb, the capital city of Croatia. we were
on our way back home to Austria. My uncle wanted to show me
where he and my mom grew up. I could see why the city was
one of the favorite cities of the Austrian/Hungarian Emperor
Franz Josef. The buildings with their ornate frescos, and
beautiful parks, were a sight to behold. Renovations are only
permitted to their original state on the outside. Inside they can
be modernized.

It was on a Sunday afternoon when my uncle told us to
stop and wait while he went ahead. He came back all excited and
took us on a side street to a five-story building where the Baptist
church was meeting on the ground floor. On the outside was a
small plaque identifying the Baptist church. The doors were
open, and we went inside to a full room of Christians, even many
young people. The front of the room was very plain with a simple
cross and the words of John 14:6 *"JA sam put, istina, I sivot."*
I am the way the truth and the life".

In my mind's eye I could see my mom and dad being
married there. The old pump organ was still in use where my

mom had played on. I was overcome by emotion, with tears streaming down my face.

It was amazing that this church had survived all those years of communism, and was still going strong. My heart was full of praise to the Lord.

My uncle told us of how he was sleigh riding down those cobblestone streets. He showed me the building where my mom was an apprentice seamstress. I could almost see my mom come out through the ornate door. My imagination was running away with me. Looking on the map, I saw the town of Blagorodovac where my Dad was born, not too far from Zagreb.

Back in Austria, my aunt found a picture with my mom and dad. Dad was holding my oldest sister Lydia, then eight months old, in his arms. My maternal grandmother was also in the picture. The picture was taken at my Star grandmother's house in front of her barn in Blagorodovac.

For years I had an unexplainable desire to know more of my father's family. My uncle and my husband decided to take me there, so back to Croatia we went.

Afraid I might be disappointed, my aunt tried to prepare me. So many years had passed, she was afraid that we might find no trace of my family. Even though I had never been there, in my mind's eyes, I could see an old, overgrown cemetery where my family was buried.

Impressed with the beauty of the country side with gentle rolling hills and fertile farmland, my heart warmed with confidence that the Lord had his hand in it, and I would find what I was looking for.

My grandmother Star was a letter carrier and had to walk five kilometers to the next town to pick up the mail. There was no post office in Blagorodovac.

My uncle was hoping to find some answers in the records of the Catholic church, for that was the only place where records were kept. But there was no church in Blagorodovac.

On the approach to the town, we saw an old overgrown cemetery just like I had pictured it. We stopped and my uncle raced ahead to search the graves for any of my family. To the right were the names of the Croatians, and to the left were the names of the Germans. Somehow, I remembered that my Star grandmother's maiden name was Sic. We found headstones on the Croatian side with that name. Then we looked at the German side and found some headstones of Star families. Some even had pictures of the person buried there. But I did not see any that I could connect with.

We drove into town and stopped at the first building, a grocery store. My uncle went inside to get some information, but the clerk had no idea. I should mention that my uncle still spoke fluently Croatian. A man across the street came out and wanted to see what the strangers were doing here. When my uncle went to speak to him, he found out that the man had bought this property from a Sic family about 45 years ago. It turned out that this was the home of my Star grandmother, the place where the picture was taken in 1938.

The house had been replaced by a new one, but the barn was still the same. The man told my uncle that there was a couple living in the last house on that street that were of German descent, and that they might know something about my grandmother.

All the houses looked alike, with a well in front, the barn on the side, and the fields in the back. When we went to that house, the man who came to the door invited us in. He said that his wife might know something. I showed Mrs. Stromeier the picture in my hand, and she pointed to my grandmother and identified her as Theresie Sic, the widowed letter carrier. She also remembered that Theresie Sic had lived in the house we had identified as the home of my grandmother. I asked Mrs. Stromeier if she knew where my grandmother was buried. She said, "Yes!" and took us to the cemetery. She pointed to a gravesite next to the one with the Sic name that we had already seen. The headstone had broken off and was gone, but Mrs. Stromeier knew that my grandmother was buried next to her brother whose grave was clearly marked.

We speculated that my grandmother must have taken back her maiden name to be able to stay in Yugoslavia.

When my mom remarried, we never spoke of my dad, so I never knew if my dad had any siblings. He was born in 1909, but I knew little else. We speculated that the First World War must have claimed his father.

I remembered that before we were to immigrate to America, a letter came from a lawyer in Yugoslavia, informing Mom that my sister Lydia, who was the oldest granddaughter, was to inherit my grandmother's estate in Blagorodovac. Mom signed off, refusing to accept it for she did not want her eldest daughter to go back to Yugoslavia.

Learning all this was definitely God's intervention and leading us. I rejoiced, praising the Lord with all my heart. What a GREAT and mighty God we have!

Chapter Eighteen
South Africa and Zambia

In October of 2003, Oskar and I were able to go on a vision trip to South Africa and Zambia, with a group of Christians led by our mission board member. My son-in-law's parents invited us to experience what the Lord was doing there. The church in Cape Town held a mission conference, and the pastor of that church was our tour guide.

We went to the Christian radio station and distributed pre-tuned solar powered radios that we brought along from America. The happy faces of the locals were worth the effort and expense. God's word goes out via the airwaves into areas where no missionary is allowed. Radio stations were being set up by our mission team, sometimes only in small huts. We were also training the local Christians to run them.

But God's Word will not return void. We were taken into shanty towns with huts made of tin and cardboards. The church was feeding children after school and giving them the gospel.

When we attended one of their services, I was awestruck by one of their songs that they sang in African. It was "When He cometh to gather His children." I had learned that song as a child in German. My son-in-law's mom sang in Norwegian, others in English, and we sang it along in our own languages.

With the help from American Christians they also built a home for Aids patients. They were not only cared for in body, but were also given the gospel to receive Jesus as their Savior. A heart rendering demonstration of love was when we laid hands on and prayed over the patients. The pastor just sobbed with emotion. Then they showed us the body tracing of the moms before they die, so the children will see the size and shape of their mom. The moms wrote precious words on the paper to their children. We walked in the prayer garden where they grew vegetables, and prayed over that ministry.

Our trip took us to Johannesburg, to Trans World Radio headquarters, and then to a resort where we went on a safari. After that we flew into Zambia. Our hotel was right at the Victoria Falls, and we were able to walk to see the falls.

It was a five-star hotel, serviced by well trained locals. The chief sold the property with the stipulation that only his people were to work there.

We took a trip into one of those villages. We saw children walking bare foot on that hot red clay. Some of them were sitting, carving African animals that were for sale. A young lady who spoke good English told us that the people once had to walk five kilometers to the Zambezi River to get water which they carried back in containers on their heads. They now have wells that were drilled by a Brother Robinson from the United States. They now have a school and receive Christian radio programs.

Our trip to South Africa and Zambia was an eye-opener.

Chapter Nineteen
Back to Europe

On a number of trips back to Austria, I've been able to enjoy the beauty of the country where we lived for twelve years in misery. Confined to refugee camps and hungry most of the time, we didn't appreciate the beauty of the land. We also, for the first time, learned about Hitler's cruelty in concentration camps.

While visiting our missionaries in upper Austria, we were able to help, hands on, at the newly established Bible school.

On a cloudy drizzling day, our missionaries, the Harveys told us of a nearby place called Mauthausen. Now a museum, it was a concentration camp during World War II. Our daughter had just graduated from high school, and was with us. We drove up to that place and my mood was like the weather.

When we entered the camp and went to the first barracks that had pictures on the wall of the prisoners, mostly children behind barbed wire, it hit me like a ton of bricks, "My God, this could have been us." I started to cry and could not stop for the next few hours. It was like a dam had broken open in me. I did not even know that there were concentration camps in Austria.

We did not learn about that in school. We were told that today every student at the age of fourteen had to go through that camp, so as to learn from the past so it would not be repeated.

As we went through the camp, we came to the ovens where so many prisoners were gassed. I could not go in. I just sat and sobbed my heart out, while my daughter and husband continued the tour. The attendant asked me why I was crying and

I was able to tell her how the Lord spared us. I was wondering how much was buried in my subconscious, that the Lord spared me from remembering. Jews were not the only prisoners and victims of the gas chambers. Gypsies, disabled people who were considered unworthy, and anyone who dared to resist the Nazi regime were there too.

We drove back to our missionaries, and I was able to relate some of our experiences.

Leaving upper Austria we drove east to the capital city of Vienna. It was no longer the bombed out city I remembered. It had been restored to its former glory.

What a wonderful time we had touring with my aunt and uncle. We drove up the highest mountain in Austria, the Grossglockner, with its road built in hairpin turns. The views were breathtaking. They took us to many different places in the Alps.

At one place we were able to view over 30 Mountain peaks over 3000 meters high. That is over 9000 feet. Each town, no matter how small, had its churches, and I loved to hear the church bells ringing. I did not know what we had missed when we lived there for twelve years, mostly in refugee camps.

*****

On a trip to Germany and Austria in 2006, we acted like American tourists with my sister Erika and her husband. We visited many famous places starting with Oberammergau, home of the world famous Passion Play. Performed on open-air stages in the village since the seventeenth century, the play portrays the crucifixion and resurrection of Jesus Christ in a dramatic way. Unfortunately for us, the presentation was only once a decade, and the next one would be in 2010. We knew that ahead of time, so we weren't surprised. It was still an interesting stop.

We rode a cable car up Zugspitze mountain, the highest of Germany's mountains. The 360-degree panoramic view was breathtaking. We could see over 400 mountain peaks in four countries.

We drove narrow, winding roads up some mountains, climbed foot paths up some, and rode cable cars up others. We rode boats with electric motors on pristine lakes deep in the forest.

We stayed in bed-and-breakfast houses for the most part, eating our meals in remote restaurants. We met my family, the Boeckels, Guettlers, and Claypools to celebrate Victor's 80th birthday.

The trip began and ended in Munich. With crowds of other tourists, we watched the Glockenspiel on the Marienplatz. High on a building wall, 32 life-sized figures dance around a circle to the music of 43 bells. The two-tiered stage comes to life every day at 11am and noon.

This was but one of our pleasure trips back to Europe. I've kept a detailed journal of each. Traveling has been a delightful part of my life, and I thank the Lord for the opportunity to see His wonders.

Chapter Twenty
Back to America

Back home in the USA, we were able to see much of our new homeland by taking a six-week camping trip across this country. This time we were pulling a pop-up trailer.

On the way to our second visit to Yellowstone National Park, we made leisurely stops at the Arch in St. Louis, the Steamboat Arabia museum in Kansas City, the Corn Palace in Mitchell, South Dakota, Mount Rushmore in Rapid City, Custer State Park in South Dakota, and Devil's Tower in Wyoming, all interesting places recommended by our good friends, Walter and Ann Berg.

Most of those places were man made, but Devil's Tower was God made, and the most awesome. The 865-foot Devils Tower can be seen from miles away. It was an incredible sight, this solid rock tower rising out of relatively flat prairie. We saw several people, like ants, climbing the vertical walls. We chose to walk the 1.3-mile hiking trail around the base. My eyes were mostly on the tower, but there were many wildflowers to enjoy on the trail. We also saw a prairie dog town, in a field dotted with the little animals standing guard on their mounds.

On our tenth day out, we arrived at Cody, Wyoming and the east entrance to Yellowstone National Park. It was quite different than our first visit 28 years ago.

We showed our Golden Age passport at the gate, and entered. What a view we had! A swiftly flowing river with snow covered mountains along the horizon. Driving along the river, we saw a bear in the distance and an elk family calmly wading in the river.

Since we had been to Yellowstone before, we decided to exit the park at the south gate and visit Grand Tetons National Park first.

The northern boundary of Grand Tetons is just four miles south of the southern boundary of Yellowstone. Moving south to the Grand Tetons was an easy move. These mountains could have been the inspiration for *"America the beautiful ... for purple mountain majesties ..."* Those purple mountains on the far side of Jackson Lake are beyond beautiful. Mount Moran is the tallest and most majestic.

The valley now covered by Jackson Lake is called Jackson Hole. The lake was so still, that the reflection of the mountains, woods, and clouds mirrored in it, made for an awesome picture. We just couldn't get enough of the view.

The lake is man-made, created by a dam across the Snake River. Otherwise, all this gorgeous scenery was God made. I enjoyed the acres and acres of wildflowers.

We drove to the town of Jackson that has a beautiful Visitor center. Interesting are the arches on all four corners of the town square that are made entirely of elk antlers.

From Teton Village we rode a gondola cable car to the top of Mount Moran. As we reached the summit, it started to snow. We couldn't see anything, so we took the cable car down again. The gift shop in Teton Village was nice, but prices were high. When we left the gift shop we looked up and saw that the snow clouds had blown away, and the summit was clear. Oh, well!

We took a boat ride across Jenny Lake, then walked a trail up to Inspiration Point. It was a steep climb, and we called it "Perspiration Point." The view of Hidden Falls was spectacular. On the way down we saw two moose cows.

Although the mighty Rocky Mountains are higher and more majestic, we still think fondly of the Austrian Alps. We called the Grand Tetons, the American Alps. There is so much to see and appreciate here. We could have used much more time.

Back in Yellowstone, we drove to the geyser basin and watched Old Faithful burst from the ground on schedule. The geyser explodes out of the ground about every 65-70 minutes. The average height of the column of water in the eruption is 130 feet, and it lasts from two to five minutes. It should be counted among the most unusual wonders of the world. People were sitting on benches awaiting the spectacular show of nature. It brought back memories of 28 years ago when we were here with Dorothy and Johnny.

We enjoyed walking the trails of Yellowstone Park again with its geysers and waterfalls and wildlife. The lower falls at the end of the Grand Canyon of the Yellowstone were said to be the most photographed waterfalls in the world. We hiked to Artist Point and had a grand view of the canyon and the magnificent waterfalls.

Mammoth Hot Springs is another wonder in Yellowstone Park. Hot water, loaded with minerals, boils up out of the ground, then cools to room temperature. The minerals then solidify and form an ever-growing mountain of terraced, multi-colored "traveltine." It's unique in its own way, but compared to the beauty we've now seen in other areas of the park, it was a bit of disappointment.

We saw lots of buffalo. We read that there are 3500 of them in the park, as well as 15 to 25 thousand elks and 610 grizzly bears and many more black bears. At one point, traffic was stopped to give right-of-way to a herd of buffalos crossing the road with their young.

The West Yellowstone KOA campground was the nicest we've seen. As I was swimming in the Olympic size swimming pool, I could look out and see the snow-covered mountains in the park. There is so much to see in Yellowstone, we felt that it would have taken our entire six weeks to see it all. The Golden Age passport allowed us to go and come into Yellowstone.

*****

Next, we pointed our car toward Glacier National Park in the northwest corner of Montana. We were warned to fill up with gas. For much of the distance there were no cars and no gas stations.

We had heard much about the magnificence of Glacier, and read that *"The grand march of the Rocky Mountains promenades the length of Montana, spilling grandeur in all directions, until they crown themselves with glory in Glacier National park."* The Park Service calls it *"the Crown of the Continent."* Now, we have found out for ourselves. It is true.

When Oskar showed our Golden Age passport and license to the ranger, he exclaimed, "I can't believe you're from Hiawassee. I'm from Ellijay, Georgia." He went on to tell us that his wife manned the gate at the western entrance to the park. They spent their summers at Glacier.

What a thrill it was crossing the mountains on the Going to the Sun Road! Parts of the road were a little scary, especially where it was cut into the side of steep cliffs. We were also a bit concerned when we had to drive through the spray of water falls, but the gorgeous scenery made the scary parts worthwhile. At Logan's Pass, at the continental divide, we drove through walls of snow, some as high as fifteen feet.

We took the boat ride across McDonald Lake and saw our first Moose grazing on the far shore.

We hiked over a hanging bridge and through the woods for almost a mile to Grinnell Lake. The beautiful clear water mirrors the high mountains with a color hard to describe. We just sat at the edge and drank in all this beauty.

We ate a snack of bananas, apples and some figs, then proceeded about a quarter of a mile to Hidden Falls. It was a very steep trail, but it was worth the effort. On our way back through the woods we admired the wildflowers, I had not seen such lush tall forget-me-nots. Suddenly, Oskar held out his arm to stop me from continuing on, for a grizzly bear and her young were coming up the path only a few yards from us. We just stood still in awe, even forgetting to take a picture, until she turned and took the horse trail and was gone in a flash.

Glacier National Park shares a portion of the U.S. border with the Waterton Lakes National Park in Canada. The two parks together have been designated the Waterton-Glacier International Peace Park, the first such park recognized by the United Nations.

We hated to leave this beautiful place.

*****

We continued the trip into Canada visiting Calgary, Banff, Lake Louise, Jasper, and the waterfalls of western British

Columbia. Back in the States, on the way home, we visited three more national parks, Bryce Canyon, Zion, and Capitol Reef.

We had spent six weeks and traveled 9,225 beautiful miles.

At other times we visited the Niagara Falls, Alaska, and the Hawaiian Islands. We are proud to be Americans. We surely feel blessed to be able to live, work and worship here.

Chapter Twenty-one
Israel

This was the trip of a lifetime, eleven days following the footsteps of Jesus and touring Old Testament sites in and around the present-day nation of Israel. The trip was a present from my husband, Oskar, for my 65th birthday.

It all began on Wednesday, March 15, 2006. We flew from Atlanta to New York, and then to Tel Aviv. My heart beat faster with excitement when we finally set foot in the Holy Land the next day. Just like David in Psalms 122: 1&2, how can I ever say thanks?

We were met at the Ben Gurion Airport by Ronny Shimon representing Morningside Tours. Ronny would be our tour guide. He proved to be an expert on all the scriptural sites in Israel, booth Old Testament and New Testament, but he told us that as a Jew he did not believe that Jesus was the Messiah.

Once all the tourists and their luggage was gathered, we boarded a comfortable motor coach for a short ride to our hotel. Dinner at the hotel was waiting, a wonderful buffet. All of our meals were excellent. It was here that we met Dr. Paul Nyquist who was to be our spiritual leader on the tour. He wanted to be called just "Paul."

The tour began at 8am Friday morning. It was a clear day as we boarded the coach destined for Caesarea by the Sea National Park. We were brought face to face with the architectural wonders of King Herod the Great.

Caesarea was founded in BC22, and was the seat of Roman government for over 500 years. Herod completely rebuilt it and named it in honor of Augustus Caesar.

In Acts 10, we read that Peter came to Caesarea in response to a vision at Joppa, and preached at Cornelius's house. In Acts 9, 18, and 21 we read that Paul visited here three times, and Acts 23 tells of Paul spending two years in prison here.

This is an underwater archeological site. Ronny told us that the deep harbor has two seawalls, one to clean itself of sand, the other to control the fresh water outlet. We also saw the aqueduct that brings fresh water ten miles from Mount Carmel.

Ascending to the summit of Mount Carmel was another experience. A statue of Elijah is at the top where he had his contest with the prophets of Baal. In the garden, Paul, our spiritual leader, brought the story of Elijah's confrontation to life. It was a story of courage. We had a great view of the Jezreel Valley. I tried to imagine how Elijah outran Ahab's chariot from here to Jezreel, told in 1Kings 18:42-46.

Mount Carmel is a wooded mountain range, triangular in shape, thirteen miles long, projecting into the Mediterranean Sea at Haifa. The mountain rises from the sea so sharply that the rapidly rising air deposits its moisture as rain or dew. We could see Mount Tabor, with Nazareth at its foot, and the whole Jezreel Valley where the battle of Armageddon will be held in the end time, Revelation16: 16.

Continuing on, we visited Megiddo, the chariot city of King Solomon. It was the most recent excavation site. Then driving up to Mount Precipice, we saw where the angry people of Nazareth tried to throw Jesus over the cliff, Luke 4:16-30.

Here again we had another great view of the Jezreel Valley, Nazareth and Mount Tabor. This mountain rises in majestic isolation from the floor of the Jezreel valley. The single peak soars to a height of 1850 feet and towers over the International Highway at the point where the highway leaves the Jezreel valley on its journey north towards the Sea of Galilee.

Mount Tabor is the traditional site of the Jesus' transfiguration, (becomes radiant in glory) although Mount Harmon may be a better candidate. In 1st Chronicles 6:77, God allotted the area of Mount Tabor as a special city for the Levites.

Driving up to Mount Arbel, we again had a magnificent view of the Sea of Galilee, with Capernaum, Magdala and Tiberias on its shores. Paul brought to our attention how small an area it was where Jesus did most of his earthly ministry, in a short time of only three years. But what an impact He made on the world for all times!

Our next destination was Tiberias, where we stayed at the grand five-star Scots Hotel. The hotel is owned and operated by the Church of Scotland, and we thoroughly enjoyed our three-night stay. Dinner was a kingly buffet with delicious food. The roasted lamb was mouthwatering, and the fresh fruits wonderful. After dinner we met in a conference room and sang hymns.

The city of Tiberius was founded by Herod Antipas in the period, 17-20AD. It was named after Tiberius Caesar the Emperor of Rome. This city is located on the western shore of the Sea of Galilee, a fresh water lake also called Lake Tiberias.

The area was known for its therapeutic hot springs, and this may explain in part why large numbers of sick people came to Jesus for healing when he was in the area. Most of Jesus' ministry was around the Sea of Galilee. In Matthew 11, Jesus pronounced judgment on several towns around the Sea of Galilee: Korazin, Bethsaida, and Capernaum. They are all gone now. Tiberias was founded after Jesus' time, and remains a blossoming city today.

On Saturday morning Oskar and I walked down to the lake and saw a wooden boat, not unlike the ones Jesus must have used. As we strolled around the garden, we felt a new kinship with our Lord.

After an amazing breakfast on the hotel terrace, we boarded a tour boat to cross the lake. To our surprise, they hoisted our American flag and played our national anthem. In the middle of the lake, the boat stopped. We reflected on the accounts of the gospels, all that had transpired here in Jesus' time.

Paul led us in devotion recounting some of the events. Here Jesus calmed the raging sea; He walked on the water; He performed the miracle of catching fish; He preached the Sermon on the Mount; He fed the multitudes; and He healed the demoniac, casting the demons into a herd of swine who hurled themselves over the cliffs of Kursi into the sea on the eastern shore.

We had a time of silent devotion, and I reflected on the Lord coming across the raging lake. I thanked Him for calming the raging sea of my life, and praised Him for being present in my life daily through the Holy Spirit.

We left the boat at the town of Gennesaret with its good view of Mount Arbel. Then we drove in our waiting motor coach up to the "mountain of the beatitudes." There is a church there, built in 1935, that has eight sides, one for the each of the eight beatitudes. The beautiful garden was perfect for our devotional time. Paul reminded us of Jesus' teaching in Matthew 5, 6, and 7, as kingdom citizens, how to live in a pagan world.

On we went to Tabgha, on the northeast side of the Sea of Galilee, to see the Church of St. Peter's Primacy. We were told that the original church was built on the site where Jesus fed the 5000 with five loaves and two fishes. This present church was constructed in 1933 over the Mensa Christi (Christ's Table) rock. There is a mosaic of loaves and fishes on the floor, and a "Nile-o-meter" measuring the water level.

Then we headed for the ruins of Korazin, just two miles from Capernaum. This was a very dangerous area prior to 1967 when Israel took back the land in the Six-Day War.

On the way to Capernaum, we had a good view of the Sea of Galilee with Mount Arbel on the other side. Ronny our tour guide told us that the Sea of Galilee was about eight feet lower than normal, and it is normally the lowest fresh water lake on planet Earth. The lack of rain and too little snow on Mount Harmon last winter were the causes.

Capernaum was our next destination. This was the hometown of Jesus, after he was rejected in Nazareth. Matthew (Levi) the tax collector was from here. More of Jesus' recorded miracles were performed in Capernaum than any other city, yet they did not believe, Matthew 11: 23-24.

Paul led us in devotions with the question, "Why Capernaum?" It was a crossroads town in a manufacturing district of Palestine. It was a blessed city in many ways. People came through from Egypt and Syria. Yet it was a cursed city because of idol worship. The people ignored Jesus' message.

An earthquake destroyed the city in 749AD, and it was never rebuilt. As we viewed the ruins, we were told that it used to be called Nahum, built in the 2nd century BC. We saw a statue of Peter and what was claimed to be the ruins of Peter's house.

We crossed the Jordan River on the Via Mare, the ancient trade route. The river was surprisingly small. We passed several mango orchards on the way to Kursi. the place where Jesus cast the demons into herd of swine that then fell over the cliffs into the sea, Luke 9. This is the only place where it could have happened. It is only here that cliffs border the lake.

Circling the Sea of Galilee, we saw that the water was somewhat choppy. Ronny explained that in afternoon, winds come from the south Mediterranean Sea and go through a gorge like a funnel. When the winds are strong, they can cause a violent storm, as is often mentioned in the Bible. The orchards we see are covered with nettings, to keep the birds out and the moisture in, protected from the sun and evaporation.

What a wonderful day this was! We had vividly relived the biblical accounts of Jesus' ministry. Praise the Lord!

It was now Sunday, the fourth day of our trip. After a big breakfast, we boarded the bus for the drive to Bethsaida. Bethsaida means house of the fisherman, and it was where Jesus found his first disciples, Peter, Andrew, James and John.

We were driving north on the International Highway that connects Egypt with Mesopotamia. From Bethsaida to the Golan Heights, passing the Old Testament city of Hazor. We drove up to the dormant volcano. What a view we had, looking at Lebanon to the west and Syria straight ahead and to the plains of Jordan.

Driving down from the mountain on a winding road we saw lots of orchards terraced into the mountain slopes. We went up to the Nimrod Fortress which was built by the Muslims, and given to the crusaders. We got a lot of history from our tour guide.

Our next stop was at Caesarea Philippi, located at the foot of Mount Hermon. Here, Paul led us through the story of Peter's confession so beautifully. Jesus asked Peter, *"Who do you say I am?"* and Peter answered. *"You are the Messiah, the son of the living God.*" After all the miracles they had witnessed, they finally understood.

Melting snow on Mount Hermon is the source of the Jordan River that feeds the Sea of Galilee. Most of the water emerges from springs at the base of the Benias cave.

We walked through the woods along the rushing waters of the Jordan River, over very rocky areas, and up to the ruins of Jeroboam's replica of Solomon's temple.

On our way back, we drove through avocado groves on both side of the highway. Ronny told us that every house in Israel has to have a bomb shelter, and each apartment a special room designed as a shelter. Each hotel has a bomb shelter too.

We were soon back at the hotel for dinner and our final night in Tiberias of Galilee.

We left Tiberias on Monday, March 20, 2006. Driving south along the Sea of Galilee, we came to the Jordan River Dam at Yardenit. This is the traditional baptismal site where many choose to follow Jesus' example of baptism in the Jordan. None of our group chose to be rebaptized. Oskar did fill a small bottle with water from the famous river as a souvenir.

We continued on to Ma'ayan Harod National Park, passing a number of kibbutz farms and orchards. This was where Gideon accepted God's call, tore down idols, and faced 135,000 Midianites with 300 Israelites chosen by God at the Gideon Spring, Judges 7 &8. This is an authentic place, the only spring and cave at the foot of Mount Bilboa. I took a picture of Oskar kneeling, pretending to lap up water from the spring. Today, this is a place where swimming pools, dressing rooms, sports equipment, and a fully air-conditioned youth hostel are provided.

Our next destination was Bet She'an National Park, an excavated city 1,000 feet below sea level at the foot of Mount

Samaria. This is where the Philistines defeated Saul's army and killed him and his son Jonathan, hanging their bodies on the wall for all to see, 1 Samuel 31:9. We climbed 150 steps up to the top of the mountain for the best view of the archeological findings of this BC fourth century activity.

The mountains of Samaria were on our left as we drove through the hills of Galilee and entered the large Jezreel valley where the Battle of Armageddon will take place. We bypassed Jericho, a political hot spot, and finally arrived at Qumran National Park, located on the northwestern shore of the Dead Sea.

Qumran's fame comes from a breakaway sect, known as the Essenes, who lived and studied here for centuries. In 1947, a Bedouin shepherd, while looking for a lost sheep, found seven ancient scrolls in a local cave. That led to a magnificent legacy, the discovery of what we now call the Dead Sea scrolls.

In another hour, we arrived at our hotel on the banks of the Dead Sea. We had a good view of Mount Nebo, the area where God buried Moses, Deuteronomy 4:6. Again, there was a magnificent buffet for dinner. Something I ate didn't agree with me though. I was sick in my room and missed an entire day of touring.

Everyone else enjoyed a tour of Masada and EinGedi and returned in the afternoon to go "swimming "in the Dead Sea. It was impossible to swim or sink. The surface of the Dead Sea is 1,412 feet below sea level. It is 997 feet deep and is almost six times as salty as the oceans. Oskar just floated around for a while to be able to say that he had done it.

We left the Dead Sea the next morning, and ascended to Jerusalem. To give us a feel of how it was in Biblical times, our driver took us on the old Jericho road. Occasionally, there were acacia trees with deep roots that reach down to underground water. Closer to Jerusalem, we saw date palm plantations.

In the days of King Herod this area was full of date palms. Presently, they have radar towers on the mountains and satellite antennae that reach outer space. There are fresh water lagoons with palm plantations around them. We were getting higher and higher into the Judean wilderness.

This was the desert where Jesus spent forty days and nights before beginning his earthly ministry. Paul led us in devotions from Psalms 121, a song of ascents.

At an overlook we could see the St. Georges Monastery and the eastern slopes of the Mount of Olives. The road became very narrow and winding, as we ascended upwards to Jerusalem.

At the foot of the Mount of Olives, we stopped and walked to the Garden of Gethsemane. "Gethsemane" means olive press. This is where Jesus was pressed to the point where his "*sweat was like drops of blood falling on the ground,*" and he prayed: "*Father, if you are willing, take this cup from me; yet not my will, but yours be done.*"

The Garden is surrounded by a wall, and a gatekeeper with a big key, let us in.

What an emotional time we had there! Paul led us to sing, "*Were you there when they crucified my Lord ...*" Oskar and I could not sing for being all choked up. It is hard to describe the emotions we experienced.

We had a group picture taken with old Jerusalem in the background with the eastern gate which was sealed by Sulaiman, a sultan of the Ottoman Empire. The Bible says that the gate will not be reopened until Jesus returns.

We then went down through the Kidron Valley and up into the old city of Jerusalem, and to the Sheraton Hotel.

The gates of Jerusalem include the Dung Gate, the New Gate, opened in 1877, the Beautiful Gate from the 16th century, the Herod Antipas Gate or the Flower Gate that leads to the Muslim quarters, the Lions Gate, the Jaffa Gate, the Zion Gate, the Golden Gate (also called the Eastern Gate), and the Damascus Gate.

Psalms 122: 1-2, *"I was glad when they said unto me, let us go into the house of the Lord...my feet shall stand within your gates O Jerusalem."*

When we walked through the Dung Gate, it took a few minutes for the realization to sink in that my feet were actually standing *"... within your gates O Jerusalem."* I was standing on holy ground. It made my heart beat faster. I had to restrain myself from falling to my knees.

Ronny said, "Welcome to Jerusalem, my home town."

*****

Now inside the old city, we took a walking tour. To reach the Temple Mount, we had to walk up a ramp to the top of Mount Moriah. The Temple Mount is a religious shrine, claimed by both Judaism and Islam. Once the location of the second Jewish temple, it now includes two Islamic buildings. We passed the Al Aqsa Mosque as we walked across a large courtyard with steps leading up to the Dome of the Rock.

The Dome surrounds the rock where Abraham was willing to sacrifice his son Isaac. This is a park like area, with places for the Muslims to wash themselves before entering the Mosque. No one is allowed to enter the Dome.

Temple Mount is enclosed by a wall that protects the 37 acre site. The Wailing Wall, or Western Wall, is believed to include a part of King Solomon's original temple. We observed a Jewish ceremony in progress when we arrived at the Wailing Wall. The area was filled with people watching the Bar Mitzvah celebration. Rams horns were blasting, and thirteen-year-old boys were loudly singing and praying as they were being carried on the shoulders of their fathers. The noise was deafening.

Oskar fulfilled a promise to a Jewish friend to place a few stones into cracks in the wall. I touched the wall and prayed for Jews to accept Jesus as their Messiah, and that peace be restored to Israel.

Paul reminded us that we were standing on the southern steps outside the wall in the area where Mary and Joseph presented eight-day old Jesus to the Temple, and where the old man Simeon took Jesus in his arms and recognized Him as the Messiah. I was overwhelmed by thoughts of many Bible stories that took place here.

Back at the hotel, we said good-bye to our marvelous tour guide Ronny. We took up a collection for him to show our appreciation. He displayed a tremendous knowledge of the Old and New Testament. I asked him if it was appropriate to wish him "May your name be written in the book of life." With tears in his eyes, he said, "Yes, very appropriate, thank you."

At the Hotel we prepared for our final day in Israel. It was Saturday, March 25th, in the year of our Lord, 2006.

As I lay awake on the last morning, reflecting on these past nine days in Israel, my mind raced. I got out of bed and looked down on Jerusalem, on the Knesset building where the Jewish parliament was meeting. I prayed for the Jewish leaders in their coming election. This was the day of Shabbat Shalom. The city was quiet and still. I prayed "May they hear the still small voice of their Messiah."

With a new tour guide, we entered the old city by way of the St. Stephens Gate walking to the Pool of Bethesda. The tradition is that the first person to enter the pool each day will be healed. There is always a race to be first. This is where Jesus healed the man who had for 38 years been paralyzed and unable to enter the pool, John 5.

We then entered the Church of St. Anne, claimed to be the birthplace of Mary the mother of Jesus. The good acoustics in this building are well known. We sang "It is well with my soul." It is located appropriately at the start of the Via Dolorosa, the road leading to the cross.

We then walked to the Antonio's Fortress, believed to be where Pontius Pilate ruled, and Jesus was tried, mocked and flogged. Then we followed along the Via Dolorosa to the Church of the Holy Sepulcher, a distance of about 2,000 feet. It was very crowded and very gaudy, people kneeling and kissing the stone where His body had been laid after He was taken off the cross.

Even the courtyard of Golgotha just seemed unreal and very disappointing with all the glitz. The only things impressive were the murals depicting the story of Jesus' death.

Then we drove to the Garden Tomb. Looking at the rock formation which resembled a skull (Golgotha means place of the skull), it was easy to assume that this was the actual tomb of Jesus. There is no proof that any of these spots are accurate, but they tell the story. It doesn't matter, because *"He is not here, for He is risen!"*

We had our own worship time in one of the assigned chapels, with singing and a communion service. The cups for the juice were made of olivewood and we were able keep them.

This was the highlight and the end of our tour. The bus took us Joppa where Jonah took the ship to flee from God. Acts

9:36 tells how Peter raised Dorcas from the dead. Peter stayed here in the house of Simon the Tanner, Acts 9:43.

We had dinner and then headed to the airport where we said our good byes.

With heart-changing memories of our walk in the footsteps of history, we returned home in the United States.

Chapter Twenty-two
Departed Loved Ones

In August of 2007, the Lord chose to take my beloved daughter Dorothy home to heaven. She was only 42, and had battled ovarian cancer for over a year. I did not want to believe that our mighty God would not heal her, for he had given her a special needs child nine years earlier.

Leaving her husband Philip and three children ages thirteen, eleven, and nine was just too hard to accept. But God chose to deliver our precious daughter from this horrific cancer, and perform the ultimate healing by taking her to heaven.

At her funeral believers and unbelievers were able to observe us as her family, as we found ourselves in the midst of the "fiery furnace" of life. Like the three Hebrews in the Old Testament. Daniel 3, *"... people could see that God was with us in the fire."* We were not burned up, but upheld by His loving arms. He will carry us through until we meet again in the presence of our Lord and Savior.

Because she accepted Jesus as her Savior at an early age, she lived for Him and loved Him. He has now taken her home to heaven, where there is no more pain, only joy in seeing her Savior's face.

At Easter before her home going she sang her last solo in her church, *"Amazing grace ... my chains are gone; I've been set free..."* Her recorded voice singing that special version of Amazing Grace was played at her funeral, accompanied by the choir. The choir members sang with tears streaming down their faces.

Music was always a special part Dorothy's life. God gave her a beautiful soprano voice that she used to glorify Him and bless us all with.

This hope of reunion is for anyone who puts their trust in Jesus. *"Because He lives, we can face tomorrow."*

*****

On August 30, 2012, Oskar, my beloved husband of 53 years, had a massive stroke, and the Lord took Him home.

Looking back on those 53 years of our marriage, I can see clearly that it was God ordained. We were both born in the former Yugoslavia, not too many miles apart. We both suffered the pain of being refugees after World War II. I've already told of the many ways God intervened to save us, then bring us together in America.

We met while singing in the choir at German Immanuel Baptist Church in New York City. He was my first and only sweetheart, and I was his. We were married in 1959.

My mother was right when she wisely compared marriage to a diamond in the rough. The more the rough edges get polished off, the more beautiful it becomes. Looking back, I would not change a thing.

Oskar loved our church, McConnell Memorial Baptist Church in Hiawassee, Georgia. We sang together in the choir, and he served as a deacon, master usher, and as a member of the Video and Television Broadcast team. Oskar loved to hear me sing solos and with my sisters as a trio.

We loved to go bowling with dear friends from our church and the bowling league.

The Lord blessed us with two wonderful children, Dorothy and John, and with five grandchildren, Daniel, Stephanie, Mary Elisabeth, Craig and Sammy.

Oskar is now free from pain and sickness, rejoicing in the presence of our Lord and Savior, and we have the blessed hope of a reunion in heaven. So, with His help we can draw strength day by day until we meet again at the feet of Jesus. *"Because He lives, I can face tomorrow."*

One of my favorite Bible verses is Isaiah 26:3, *"You will keep in perfect peace those whose minds are steadfast, because the trust in you."*

Praise be to God!

Chapter Twenty-three
Second Trip To Israel

In January of 2019, I traveled to Israel for the second time, this time with Johnny, Lisa and eleven-year old Sammy. Sammy was excited, and I was anxious for them to experience "Walking in the footsteps of Jesus" in Israel.

We were met at the Tell Aviv airport by our tour guide, Uncle Kenny. The nice motor coach was driven by Josi. We were presented with ear buds so that we could hear his presentation. We were tired from the long airplane ride, but there was to be no rest. It was the morning of the Sabbath, and we could not check in to the hotel in Tiberias until later. So, instead of relaxing at the hotel, we started right away on the tour.

I described many of the points of interest in my account of our 2006 trip, so, in most cases, I won't repeat the details.

Our first stop was at Caesarea on the coast of the Mediterranean Sea. The city boasts of the largest harbor on the Mediterranean. It was the home of Pontius Pilate. We sat on the steps of an ancient amphitheater facing the sea for our first devotions. Pastor Gary, from Johnny's church in Cashiers, NC, served as our spiritual guide.

Next, we drove to Mount Carmel where the prophet Elijah confronted the prophets of Baal. Sammy remembered the Bible story of Elijah outrunning the chariot of King Ahab and wondered how that could be. I directed him to 1 Kings 18:46 that states that the hand of God was on Elijah. Mount Carmel was also where Elisha went with the Shunammite woman to bring back her son from the dead.

At the top of Mount Carmel we had a great view of the Jezreel valley where the battle of Armageddon will take place, Revelations 16:16.

The Lake House in Tiberias at the Sea of Galilee was now ready for us. It was a welcome site for us weary travelers. After dinner every one retreated to their rooms for a good night's sleep.

The Sea of Galilee is really just a large lake, fed from melting snow from mountains in the north and draining via the Jordan River to the Dead Sea in the south. It was the area where Jesus performed many of His miracles.

On the second day we visited Meggido. King Solomon's chariot city, and Magdala, the home of Mary Magdalene. We also visited the Church of the Primacy in Tabgah by the Sea where Jesus fed the 5,000 with five loaves and two fish. The mosaic on the floor depicts the event.

Seven springs of warm water makes this a good fishing spot. One of Jesus' miracles was directing the unsuccessful fishermen to lower their nets on the opposite side of the boat. The result was more fish than they could handle without sinking the boat. Sammy, my little fisherman, could picture it happening.

At a charcoal fire near this spot, Peter was reminded of his denial of Jesus. This time Jesus asked Peter three times, "Do you love me?" Peter replied, "You know that I do." Jesus then restored him for his future ministry.

The highlight of our third day was the ceremonial baptisms in the Jordan River. Twelve of our group, including Lisa and Sammy, were baptized, several for the first time. What a blessing it was to see Pastor Gary pray over each candidate. It was an emotional time as some left their "baggage" from the past in the river.

The next day we walked in heavy rain down to the lake shore to board a ship, not unlike the one Jesus used. The captain was a Messianic Jew who gave his testimony and led the singing of beautiful hymns in English and in Hebrew. Just like thirteen years ago, the American flag was raised as we sang our national anthem.

In the center of the lake the boat stopped, and we had our devotions. I was taken back to the many times in my life when Jesus stilled the storms of my life, first as a refugee, then my daughter was taken home to heaven, and the home going of Oskar. I could sense of the presence of the Lord and praised Him for always being with my through the Holy Spirit.

At the far side of the lake, we visited the Yigel Allon Center which was devoted to the man of Galilee. A 2,000 year old boat was on display. A film showed the interesting story of the boat's excavation.

We visited the Church of the Beatitudes where Jesus gave his Sermon on the Mount, then went to Nazareth, the boyhood home of Jesus, and to Bethsaida where Jesus enlisted his first disciples, Peter, Andrew, James, and John.

Nazareth is the largest city in the northern district of Israel, also known as the Arab capital of Israel. Nazareth Village is a living replica of the time of Jesus. The life-sized display included such things as terraced vineyards, an ancient wine press, stone quarries, a watch tower over the vineyards, an olive press, a village well, a thrashing floor, and a tomb where Sammy entered and looked around. The residents were wearing native costumes. There were shepherds tending live animals. There also was a synagogue where a tour guide read from a scroll. It was an interesting place that set us back in time.

It was still raining heavily when we returned to our hotel in Tiberias, but the next day we awoke to sunshine. We drove up to Mount Bental, one of the highest peaks in the Golan Heights. The Golan Heights is a ridge that is 49 miles long at an elevation of 2,700 feet. On top of a dormant volcano is old army outpost with underground bunkers that we entered.

The view from here was incredible, looking down into Syria and the Damascus Road where Jesus appeared to Saul of Tarsus in a bright light that blinded him, Acts 9:1-9.

Our next visit was to Ceasarea Philippi on the slopes of Mt. Harmon, where the Jordan River begins. At Tell Dan archeologists have excavated the ruins of this historic city of refuge. An altar with four horns gave Sammy a challenge as he climbed to touch the horns. We stopped at the 4,000-year old Abraham's Gate. Moses' father-in-law Jethro was said to have been buried there.

At the Benais River National Preserve, we went on a very strenuous hike along the rushing river. The waterfall at the end of the trail was the tallest in all of Israel.

The next morning we left Galilee and headed south toward the Dead Sea.

Our next stop was at Bet Shean National Park to see the excavated ancient city of Decapolis, 1000 feet below sea level. This is where the Philistines defeated Saul and his army. He and his son Jonathan were killed and their heads hung out for all to see, 1 Samuel 31:9&10.

We walked on the actual streets made of mosaic with genuine colors of the stones. Sewer lines run in the middle of the streets. The monumental colonnade running along Sylvanus street, the Roman theaters, the bath houses were all very interesting. Lisa and some of our group hiked up the 150 steps overlooking the best site of archaeological findings from the 4th century BC.

We stopped at the National Preserve of Ma'ayan Harod (means fear) at the foot of Mount Gilboa. This was where Gideon accepted God's call, tore down idols, and faced 135,000 Midianites with 300 Israelites chosen by God at the Gideon Spring, Judges 7 &8. This is an authentic place, the only spring and cave at the foot of Mount Bilboa. Johnny and Sammy knelt by the spring pretending to lap up water just as Oskar had done thirteen years earlier. Today, this is a place where swimming pools, dressing rooms, sports equipment, and a fully air-conditioned youth hostel are provided.

We were driving into the wilderness of Samaria, passing a checkpoint into the Judean desert. There were lots of date palms that reminded me of the prophesy of Isaiah 35:1 that the desert will bloom again. In modern times, they reclaim the desert by irrigation. From here we could see Jericho, the oldest city of that area. It is below sea level. It was under Palestinian control, so we could not go there. This the area where Elijah ascended in a fiery chariot, 2 Kings:2.

Jericho reminded us of Zacheus and the sycamore tree. Remembering that story, Sammy found a sycamore tree and climbed it. I took his picture up in the tree.

At Gilgal we were reminded of the miracle of crossing the Jordan River on dry ground as recorded in Joshua 4:19 – 5:12. Gilgal was where God ceased providing the Israelites with manna.

To the east we got our first look at the Dead Sea. It was choppy and much too rough for a swim. Lisa took Sammy down to the water's edge. I went for a swim in the hotel's swimming pool. A severe sand storm came from the desert. While at dinner at the hotel Le Meridian David, an unusually heavy rain and thunderstorms caused a power failure.

Because of the storms, we missed seeing Qumran Caves where the Dead Sea scrolls were found. However, we were able to view some of the scrolls at the Shrine of the Book museum in Jerusalem. We were told that it had snowed here the day before.

It was also disappointing to me that Sammy didn't get to see the Judean wilderness where Jesus spent 40 days fasting in the desert. It was also where the story of the Good Samaritan took place, Luke 10:25.

Because of flooded roads we had to take a detour that took us through the northern Negev peninsula known for its abundance of natural gas. We missed Hebron, the area where Abraham and the patriots were buried.

Settling in on the sixteenth floor of the Plaza Hotel in Jerusalem, we had a good view of the city at night. Sammy and I went for a swim in the hotel pool, while Johnny and Lisa spent some time with friends.

The next day the Lord blessed us with sunshine, but it was cool. At the Mount of Olives, we had our group picture taken with the golden Dome of the Rock in Jerusalem in the background.

I was impressed as I looked at the wall surrounding Jerusalem and seeing the closed Eastern Gate. I remembered that some day it would be opened when Jesus returns. I pictured in my mind Jesus coming down from the upper room, crossing the Kidron Valley and up to this place, only 1000 feet, just a Sabbath days walk.

Our visit to the Garden of Gethsemane was heartwarming and emotional. This was the spot here Jesus, anticipating the agony and ordeal ahead of him, was so pressed he sweated drops of blood, Luke 22:44. At the gate we were met by the gatekeeper who unlocked the gate with a large key to let us in. We had a devotion time with Pastor Gary, then we went to separate trees to pray individually. One of the trees was old enough to have been there with Jesus. It was protected by wire. Pastor Gary went from person to person laying hands on each and praying for each of us. Lisa and I chose a spot in view of the Eastern Gate. Johnny and Sammy chose a bench next to us.

Back on the bus, we drove through the Kidron Valley up to the City of David, now under Muslim control. We could hear the haunting sounds of the Muslim call to prayer. We went through the Warren Shaft where David's men entered and conquered the city, 2 Samuel 5:8. We exited the shaft at the Pool of Siloam where the blind man washed his eyes which had been healed by Jesus, John 9:7.

On the Sabbath day, in the hotel dining room we were blessed by a Jewish family with their three young children at our table. The father led the family in their Sabbath prayers, and read the Shema from Deuteronomy 6:4-9. We had a nice conversation with them. The wife was from Russia, and the husband was born in Israel. I blessed them with *"May your name be written in the Book of Life."*

After breakfast on the next day we drove over to the Knesset where the parliament of Israel is located. We viewed the giant menorah which was a gift of the British.

Passing a number of gates in the old wall, we drove to the Shepherds Field overlooking Bethlehem (House of Bread), the birthplace of Jesus. Sadly, we were unable to enter Bethlehem because it is under Palestine control.

Our next destination was the Herodium, which was King Herod's man made mountain. We had a steep climb from the parking lot to the top of the mountain and down through the water shaft, at times on a spiral staircase. At a checkpoint a Palestinian soldier with a machine gun boarded our bus for inspection. There were numerous signs prohibiting entry to the Palestinian side.

We stopped at the American Embassy, with its large emblem of the United States of America, just recently moved here from Tel Aviv. On our way to our tour guide's home in a kibbutz, we passed through the Sorek Valley where David killed Goliath, 1 Samuel 17. Chuck Swindoll was quoted that *"Goliath was pretty big in size, but he was dwarflike compared to God who empowered David."*

Kenny took us to his kibbutz, a community in Israel traditionally based on agriculture. He showed us around for us to see life in a kibbutz today. We planted two trees in a very muddy field. Then he took us to his house and introduced us to his wife. She had prepared refreshments of pastries, almonds, dates, nuts and hot tea. There were 500 members of this kibbutz, 150 families living on 6,000 acres of land. All residents were Jewish and had to be voted in.

Back at the hotel I soaked my tired feet and body in a bubble bath.

We visited the Temple Mount and the Dome of the Rock. At the Wailing Wall, I have a beautiful picture of Sammy praying at the wall. We heard comments about the museum for the future third temple, where furniture and fixtures for the temple are stored. A farm in the United States is breeding the red heifer for the temple.

We toured David's tomb and the Upper Room where Jesus ate his Last Supper. After the resurrection Jesus met with his disciples twice in the Upper Room.

At the exit of the Zion Gate we saw busloads of military recruits, young men and women. Sammy shook hands with some of them. One of them looked just like his big brother, Craig, who was in the army in Oklahoma.

Back at the hotel Sammy and I went to the pool for an hour and a half swim.

On the last day of our trip to Israel, the heavens declared the glory of God. The Lord blessed us with sunshine again.

Back to the old city, we entered Herod's Gate and visited the Praetorium where Pontius Pilate condemned Jesus to die on the cross. It was my sin that nailed Him to the cross, and His great love that held Him there. His resurrection gives us hope.

We walked the Via Delarosa, the way to the cross. We entered the Church of the Holy Sepulcher and climbed the steps to the spot claimed to be the location of the cross. Lastly, we went to the supposed tomb. The glitz of it all turned me off, just as it had thirteen years ago. What does it matter? HE IS NOT HERE, HE IS RISEN.

Our driver had the motor coach ready to take us to the Garden Tomb near Golgotha, a rock formation that looks like a skull. This was where Stephen, the first Christian martyr, was stoned.

We walked through the garden to get to the tomb. Then we were able to enter the tomb. They don't claim that this was the actual tomb, but this made more sense to me as being the actual tomb where Jesus was laid before rising again on the third day.

We had our worship service and communion in a special place provided and were praising our risen Lord.

At the Holocaust Museum, called Yat Vashem, the children's memorial made a lasting impression on Sammy. Johnny took him under his wings to explain the tragedy reflected there. At the memorial the names of the 1,500,000 children who were murdered were spoken out loud in the darkness.

At the airport we said goodbye to Kenny and Josi, our tour guide and driver, and to some of our group who took different planes. Our plane was huge and much nicer than the one we came on. With extra leg room, we were able sleep some during the eleven-hour return flight. Still, it was a long flight home.

Home at last, I prayed for Johnny and his family, that the Israel experience would give them better insight to the scriptures, and reward them with a closer relationship with the Lord.

Afterword

The Lord is still working in my life, day by day, and I praise HIM for being my heavenly Father. Looking back, I can see God's hand in everything that has happened to me and my family. I look forward to walking hand in hand with my Father in the years to come, until He calls me home.

It is my prayer that the reader can see my heavenly Father's hand leading me throughout my life.

Made in the USA
Columbia, SC
17 August 2019